Family Law Made Simple

Marriage, Divorce, Children, Separation & The Legal System

Slater & Gordon

Published by: [WP] Wilkinson Publishing Pty Ltd   ACN 006 042 173

Level 4, 2 Collins Street, Melbourne, Vic 3000
Tel: 03 9654 5446, www.wilkinsonpublishing.com.au
Copyright © 2014 Slater & Gordon Limited. All rights reserved.

Cataloguing-in-Publication data:
Author: Slater & Gordon.
Title: Family law made simple : marriage, divorce, children,
                                 separation & the legal system.
ISBN: 9781922178268 (paperback)
Subjects: Domestic relations.
                                 Marriage law. Families.
Dewey Number: 346.015
Cover Design: David Shaw, Home Creative   Layout: Chris Georgiou

FOREWORD

Years of experience in both the UK and Australia has taught the lawyers at Slater & Gordon that many people find it hard to navigate their way through the legal system. Slater & Gordon have spent the last 85 years helping people understand their rights and how the law works during what are often the toughest periods of their lives.

Going through a divorce or separation is normally one of those tough periods and the process of navigating your way through a complex legal system can be overwhelming and confusing.

This book is designed to explain in simple, impartial terms what your rights are and what steps you need to take during this time and will hopefully provide support and advice in how to successfully work your way through the legal maze of family law and start moving on with the next stage of your life.

This guide focuses on the essential aspects of the law that people need to know when going through a relationship breakdown as well as outlining how the process will work, step by step. It talks you through the obstacles you will face on the journey and provide you with advice on how to overcome them as well as dispelling the many myths surrounding family law.

The authors are all practising lawyers in the Slater & Gordon family law team and as well as having a full understanding of the stress involved in a relationship breakdown they have first-hand experience of the scenarios contained in this book.

There is never a substitute for a good family lawyer but this guide should provide you with the information you need to make the process as easy as possible.

We hope it will give you the insight and knowledge to confidently negotiate the intricacies of the legal process and move on with your life confident that the outcome was fair and reasonable and in keeping with the law.

The Family Law Team
Slater & Gordon

ACKNOWLEDGEMENTS

Slater & Gordon would like to thank the members of the family law team who worked tirelessly on producing *Family Law Made Simple.*

Particular thanks go to our key contributor Sarah Thompson. Sarah is a Principal Lawyer in the UK Family department of Slater & Gordon as well as being a trained mediator and collaborative lawyer. Sarah's career has spanned over 15 years and her extensive experience in all areas of matrimonial and family law, coupled with her reputation as a robust advocate, attracts a range of clients, from those with modest assets to Captains of Industry and sports personalities. Sarah's efforts and dedication to the book were unparalleled.

Sarah Thompson

CONTENTS

INTRODUCTION

Everybody knows someone who is separating or divorcing. It is a fact of life in the UK today. Getting into a relationship is relatively easy. However, whether you are married or just living with your partner, leaving that relationship may be a difficult experience – especially if you have children or you can't agree over the distribution of your property.

This book provides useful and practical information for those who find themselves involved in the family law process. It is written for those who do not know, or are unsure, what that law is and how it is applied. It is written by family lawyers who deal with these issues every day and have a wealth of experience and who can help you avoid the pitfalls and realise when you may need to ask for professional help.

There are several pieces of legislation that come under the umbrella of family law as well as numerous cases that guide and direct parties to litigation, and lawyers and judges to a conclusion. The main statutes are as follows:

1.   The Matrimonial Causes Act 1973 – which sets out what the law is in relation to married couples and those in a civil partnership who seek a divorce or dissolution.

2.   The Children Act 1989 – which sets out what the law is in relation to the children of either married or unmarried parents, grandparents and other carers of children.

3.   The Trusts of Land and Appointment of Trustees Act 1996 – which sets out the law in relation to property owned by various categories of people who are not married or in a civil partnership. This can include parents contributing to the purchase of a property to be lived in by their child.

This book tells you in very simple language what the law is, how it operates and how it might affect you if you have a breakdown in your relationship.

It takes you through the steps from separation until it's all over, there's even a chapter on life after divorce, all explained in plain English.

The book is relevant for all couples, whether married, unmarried, heterosexual or homosexual.

This book came about after a realisation that many people don't really understand what family law is about and how it might apply in their specific circumstances. Even fewer understand how legal fees and costs are calculated and charged, and what the potential financial obligations might be.

Not all lawyers use plain language to explain the legal process or the options available. Some lawyers also aren't good at discussing with clients the costs for their services. This book explains family law and cost issues, step by step, in everyday language. It explains the reality of legal costs and family law and the steps you can take to minimise or, at the very least, contain and control costs. This information could save you money that would otherwise end up in the pockets of lawyers or wasted on experts telling you what you already know.

This book provides a guide to:

▸ The legal principles when children are involved

▸ What is a fair and reasonable property settlement

▸ How to resolve matters as amicably as possible

▸ The legal and court processes, step by step

▸ What to consider when deciding whether you need a lawyer

▸ How to find the right lawyer, what questions you should ask and how to instruct them

▸ How to get certainty and contain your legal costs

We don't pretend to give you all the legal possibilities and all of the answers. This book does not provide legal advice and is not intended as a substitute for legal advice. However, it is a guide that will help you to negotiate the processes involved and find appropriate advice when it might be needed.

The law is correct as at January 2014.

WHEN IT'S OVER, IT'S OVER – WHAT DO YOU DO NOW?

SUMMARY

▶ Think seriously about whether or not to leave a relationship.

▶ If you intend to leave, consider how you will leave, what you will take with you, what will happen to your children and the effect on your financial situation.

▶ Even if you think that the relationship is over, should you leave at all? There are the practical implications of where you will live. In the longer term, you may lose control over issues such as selling the property.

▶ Before you leave, make sure you have copies of all your important documents, as well as photographs of valuable assets such as artwork and furniture.

▶ When you leave, take with you any items of personal importance. You may never see them again otherwise.

▶ Remember that every case is different – whatever the outcome in your sister's divorce, or your workmate's separation, it is unlikely to be the same for you.

▶ You do not have to leave your home to separate from your partner. But if you are married and seeking to rely on separation in your divorce, you will need to be able to evidence that you are living completely separately, albeit under the same roof.

▶ Stay safe. If you fear abuse or violence, there are many resources listed in this book to help. Remember, not all abuse is physical violence – abuse can be emotional or financial.

▶ Consider talking to a lawyer to figure out what your options are and where you stand. Even if you do not want to engage a lawyer throughout the process, it may help at the start so that you can get your questions answered.

Leaving a relationship is not an easy decision

To stay in a relationship or to go is not a decision to make lightly, especially if you have children.

Whether you are in a marriage or cohabiting, once you have made the decision to separate – but before you actually do – you should plan your course of action. Naturally, you will need to work out where you will go and when, and you will also need to consider with whom and what you will take with you. You might consider questions such as:

▸ Will you take the children?

▸ What about the pets?

▸ Do you fear a violent response? And how you can keep yourself safe.

▸ Can you take the company car?

▸ Does your departure create any legal implications?

It is important to get proper advice on these issues before you go, because your decisions may have unforeseen consequences that could cause problems for you in the future. If you are uncertain, seek assistance or support from one of several government agencies, counselling services or groups who can provide help. Most are either free or are reasonably priced and cost effective.

Some of these resources are set out in the pages that follow. Even if a particular resource is not relevant for you, they will at least give you guidance and point you in the direction of resources that are more appropriate for your situation.

Counselling services

There are many counselling services that can help you – they are too numerous to list here, but a simple Internet search will produce details of counselling services in your area. The Citizen's Advice Bureau can also offer free independent advice and are a good port of call for your more general enquiries.

You also need to determine whether you need to get legal advice at this stage (see chapter 9 'Lawyers – finding the right ones and working with them').

Making sure you have the information

When you separate, make sure you have access to information and documentation that may be useful to help resolve issues that arise further down the track. This information could be invaluable evidence if things can't get resolved sensibly.

For example, if you have a dispute over property, you will need to have access to information that might help a court to determine answers to the following questions:

▸ What are your assets and liabilities?

▸ Who made what contribution to those assets and liabilities during your relationship and before you got together?

▸ What are your employment arrangements?

▸ Do either of you (or the children) have significant health issues?

▸ What are the care arrangements for your children?

Think about the information that might be available to you before you separate. Make a list of all of the assets in the home. If possible, take dated photographs of each room. Take photos of paintings, jewellery, antiques and any other precious items you may have. This will help demonstrate that the particular assets existed at that date (or use the age-old technique of including the front page of a newspaper in your photos). Take photographs of the inside of properties and gardens, to prove what condition they were in when you separated. You might be surprised how quickly people's recollections change on how well (or badly) properties have been maintained.

You are entitled to take with you all of your own documents, including details of, say, a joint account (provided yours is one of the names on the account). If you can't or don't want to take them with you then you should copy or scan as many documents as you can, including:

▸ Mortgage, lease or loan contracts.

▸ Bank and credit card statements, cheque and receipt book butts.

▸ Letters from business associates, financiers, banks, accountants or lawyers.

3

▸ Receipts for major items such as school fees, travel, furniture, electronics, building work and supplies, insurance.

▸ Pay slips, P60's, tax returns, information about pensions, and

▸ Shareholding portfolios and property investments.

If you can't copy or scan documents, take a blank deposit form or a cheque to identify the bank and the branch where the accounts are held.

CAUTION – VERY IMPORTANT

However, you must not under any circumstances take a copy of any documents on which you are not named whether they are in your spouse's sole name or joint names with another party or which belong to your spouse. As tempting as it might be, you would be severely criticised and would be liable to incur penalties later on. There are exceptions to this, but don't rely on these unless you have taken legal advice on this particular point – your spouse has a right to privacy even if you live together.

Before separation – a bit of preliminary advice might help

When relationships are going through a bad patch, there is usually a lot of support and advice from the sidelines. Family and friends are there to help and often feel they are competent to advise you on what to do (or what not to do). However, the experiences of your sister-in-law, who was left by her husband five years ago and who had to fight tooth and nail for residence of the children, may not be relevant to your situation. The fact that your best friend got 65 per cent of the property distribution does not mean that you will.

Every case is different in family law. No two situations are the same. 'This is what happened' stories in family law matters are often distorted, one-sided or simply fail to mention matters that may have had a significant impact on the result.

Your family or friends can provide emotional support at this time but they are unlikely to be able to contribute much information of real value about family law and how it works, so be careful before acting on their advice on legal issues. It may well be inaccurate and cause more problems than are solved.

The breakdown of a relationship of any sort is usually very emotional. However, emotional issues – no matter how strongly you feel about the treatment you may have received, or the injustice of what your former partner has done – should not be allowed to cloud the real reason that you are getting legal advice. You have a legal problem to resolve and it will be resolved faster (and at less cost) if you stick to the facts of the matter and work towards resolution rather than apportioning blame.

A lawyer will stand back from the emotion, look at the facts and apply their knowledge and experience to advise you on what should be done. However, they can put you in contact with a counsellor for psychological and emotional support to help you through these difficult times if that is what you need.

It is important when you are going through the trials of a separation or divorce that you seek independent professional advice, at least about:

▶ Family law as it applies to your specific circumstances.

▶ The legal processes you may have to go through.

▶ Your options and which course of action might be appropriate, and

▶ The costs and expenses involved and if a fixed fee approach would be suitable.

Initial legal advice will usually be quite inexpensive (many family lawyers offer free first consultations) and it should give you a basic understanding of the system, what to expect and how much it's all going to cost. A good lawyer should also alert you to potential pitfalls and help you avoid making decisions you might regret later. Your lawyer can often point you in the right direction for any additional assistance you might require.

What is 'Separation'?

Separation is a state of fact. You do not have to make a sworn statement or file documents in court to separate. Although it may have legal consequences, there is no such thing in England and Wales as a 'legal separation'.

The simplest demonstration of separation is for one party to move out, or for you both to decide to live completely separate lives albeit under the same roof. This means more than just having separate bedrooms; you need to do your own shopping, cleaning and cooking.

Physical separation, when one person leaves the home, is the most obvious evidence of an intention to end the relationship. It is also much easier to divorce on the grounds of, say, 2 years separation if you are not living in the same house.

Interim financial arrangements

When you separate from your partner, you will need to consider the following points:

- If you are married, do you need money to support yourself while you sort out the final settlement? This could be just for everyday living or to pay your lawyers. NB. Spousal Maintenance is not available if you are not married.

- Do you need money to support your children? You can apply for Child Maintenance regardless of whether you are married or not.

- Are you worried your ex is going to sell the house from under you? See Injunctions to preserve property below.

Interim Spousal Maintenance

If you are struggling to make ends meet because you have split up with a partner (i.e. spouse or civil partner, but not if you were cohabiting) you may be able to obtain an order for Interim Spousal Maintenance from the courts. Interim Spousal Maintenance orders will not be made in every situation.

The test to determine whether you should receive (or pay) financial support is in two parts. Firstly, is there a shortfall between your income from all sources (including salary and benefits) and your reasonable outgoings? The key word here is "reasonable". It would include items such as rent or mortgage, utility bills, food, and necessary travel (e.g. for work). It no longer includes an amount for your legal fees (but you can now apply to the court for an interim payment from your partner to help cover your legal fees, known as a Legal Services Order), and would not normally include non-essential items such as your gym membership. Calculate what you need to "keep the ship afloat" while you sort out the other issues, such as what happens to the house and how are you going to divide any capital. The second step is whether the payer is reasonably able to pay. For more details, look at section 22 of the Matrimonial Causes Act 1973 (as amended).

Spousal Maintenance (other than Interim Spousal Maintenance) is discussed in chapter 4.

If you were living together, but were not married or in a civil partnership, you are not eligible for any form of spousal maintenance.

Child Maintenance

You can seek financial support for children in your care and for whom you receive Child Benefit (if you are eligible for Child Benefit) by either agreeing between yourselves what Child Maintenance your ex will pay, or in the absence of an agreement, by applying to the Child Maintenance Service (CMS), formerly known as the Child Support Agency. The CMS has a very good online calculator that will give you an idea as to how much is likely to be paid in your particular set of circumstances. You do not need to have been married or in a civil partnership to receive Child Maintenance; the fact you have a child together is sufficient.

If the CMS does not have jurisdiction, e.g. when the paying party doesn't live in the UK, then you will have to look outside the CMS for help. This can be complicated and you are likely to need a lawyer to help you.

If you have an ex-partner who earns a very high income, then you may be able to apply to court for a top up of Child Maintenance.

Injunctions to freeze assets

In this context, an injunction is an order from a court that says STOP! You might, for example, get an injunction to prevent your ex-partner from selling off or disposing of assets that you have an interest in. This extends to selling a house, shares or any other asset. The injunction will protect the property or asset until the court determines (or you agree) how much money and which items you will keep or what will be sold.

Once you have separated

Once you have separated, you can make arrangements for the distribution of your property and the living and time-sharing arrangements for your children – unless you have been able to sort it all out before separating.

Property and children's arrangements may be finalised by coming to an agreement with your ex, or you can make an application to a court.

You could say goodbye, shut the door behind you then head straight down to the court to lodge an application. However this is usually not the best option. The process of getting sound advice and deciding what to do next requires cool, calm consideration.

In many cases, there is no great urgency to resolve matters. In others, there may be reasons to get things moving, such as protecting your children or ensuring assets are not sold or thrown away. Either way, it is wise to get some professional advice about your position and how best to move forward.

You may need to engage a lawyer at this point, or simply get some preliminary advice to help you to work out your own resolution. If you have not obtained advice before separation, you certainly should do so soon afterwards. Your lawyer is there to give you advice and, if you choose to retain him or her, must act on your instructions.

Getting legal advice is not an aggressive or hostile thing to do, although many people see it that way when they discover their ex-partner has visited a lawyer. There is absolutely no reason why people who are separated (or in the process of separating) should not seek independent legal advice about their position and how to deal with matters properly. Failing to get advice is a bit like hopping behind the wheel of a car without ever having learned to drive. You've seen other people do it, many of your friends may have told you about it, but you have never driven a car before – it might be sensible to get a few hints about driving, so you can avoid the risk of crashing at the first bend!

If circumstances permit, be open. Tell your ex-partner that you are simply trying to find out how to do things properly. What is important at this stage is that you are aware of your rights and responsibilities and have a practical framework within which to deal with the end of your relationship.

It is worth bearing in mind that:

▶ You do not have to have a disagreement with your ex-partner over what is going to happen with the children.

▶ You do not have to engage in a legal battle over the assets (or what will be left of them after you pay the legal expenses).

▶ You do not have to go to court.

However, what you really should do is find out where you stand and get some legal advice on your options and the best way to move forward.

Violence and abuse

You may be forced to leave home suddenly because of violence or abuse.

Abuse takes many forms. It can be physical, sexual, emotional, financial or a combination of any or all. None are acceptable in our society.

If you are the victim of violence, or have a real fear of violence occurring, contact a lawyer, and if necessary, contact the police. However, be absolutely sure that your claims are soundly based and are not just a means of getting back at your partner. The courts strongly disapprove of false allegations about a violent partner that have been made up in order to gain some other advantage (such as sole occupation of the home or restrictions on contact with children). False claims of violence are a gross abuse of the legal process and can result in a Costs Order being made against you.

There are organisations that provide support and assistance to victims of abuse or violence. Your lawyer can provide you with a list of relevant bodies in your area or you can find them on the Internet.

If you have been abused in any way, note the details, including the time and date of the incidents and whether anybody else was present. Try to note what was said. If you have suffered injury, consult a doctor and ask for a report. Obtain photographic evidence where appropriate. Make a report to the police.

Your personal safety is paramount and you should do everything in your power to avoid situations that may lead to abuse. Regrettably, all too often this is not possible.

IN CONCLUSION:

▶ Obtain legal advice before starting detailed negotiations about property. You may make an agreement that is unfair to you without knowing it.

▶ Don't try to prevent your children from having contact with their other parent unless there are issues of violence or abuse.

▶ Visit your children's school and speak to teachers to let them know the separation has occurred. Schools need to know so that they can help monitor the children's adjustment to separation. It is also a good idea to provide them with your contact details so any letters, reports etc. can also be copied to you.

▶ Keep a diary. If a matter proceeds to court, you may need to prepare a statement detailing issues relating to the children's arrangements. People often find it difficult to remember timelines and dates. Keeping a diary will make it easier. Include notes about contact dates with your children, even those that are missed.

▶ Talk to friends and family members for support.

▶ Get professional help to deal with the emotional fall-out – for example, from a psychologist.

▶ Be open minded about counselling for yourself and for your children. Even if your ex-partner is reluctant to attend counselling, you may find it very helpful to attend on your own.

UNDERSTANDING THE BASICS OF THE LAW

SUMMARY

▸   Family law need not be overly complicated.

▸   The objectives of family law are straightforward:

  ▸   to protect the best interests of any children, and

  ▸   to provide for a fair split of your property.

▸   Most of the time, there are two options when your relationship is over – settle matters between you, or take your case to court and fight over who gets what.

▸   Going to court is very expensive and can be a very negative process.

▸   The requirement for obtaining a divorce is very straightforward – there must have been an irretrievable breakdown of the marriage.

▸   If you are in a relationship and live together, (including if your relationship is a same-sex relationship), then unless you have undergone a marriage or civil partnership ceremony, you are not considered 'married' in the eyes of the law. There is no such thing as a 'common-law' wife or husband.

▸   If you are cohabiting and you break up, the court will treat your relationship differently to a marriage. Dividing up your assets will be dealt with very differently.

▸   Children of cohabiting couples are however covered by The Children Act, which is the same law as for children of married couples.

What Family Law is… and is not

Family law need not be complex or difficult. Basically, it deals with issues around children and property (financial matters) after you have separated.

The law provides for:

▶ What happens after you separate (whether married or in a civil partnership).

▶ How you divide up what was previously owned by both of you, and

▶ How arrangements are made for your children (including Child Maintenance).

The Matrimonial Causes Act 1973 was passed to provide guidance regarding the factors a court should consider upon the breakdown of a relationship, to enable people to get on with their lives after separation.

Since 1973, the Matrimonial Causes Act (as amended) has become a much more complex set of laws. But the bottom line remains: the law is in place to enable people who have separated to resolve the distribution of their property on a reasonable basis.

The interests of children were looked at in detail and embodied in statute in the Children Act 1989, which was considered to be groundbreaking legislation at the time. This statute introduced the concept of 'Parental Responsibility' for children and established the type of court orders that parents could apply for in relation to their children, upon separation. It also established the 'Welfare Principle', to ensure that the welfare of the children would always be the court's paramount consideration.

In 2004 the law developed further, with the passing of the Civil Partnership Act, to allow same-sex couples to gain the same rights as married heterosexual couples, by undergoing a Civil Partnership ceremony. The Act also set out how the law would be applied to these couples upon any separation and dissolution of the Civil Partnership. In 2013 the law relating to same sex couples came into line with heterosexual couples with the passing of The Marriage (Same Sex Couples) Bill. This means that from 13th March 2014 same sex couples can now be married.

What the Law covers

The objectives of the law are to ensure that the best interests of children are protected and that proper financial arrangements are made for the division of property. The Matrimonial Causes Act 1973, the Civil Partnership Act 2004, the Children Act 1989 and the decisions of the Family Courts set out the principles and rules for resolving these issues and other matters that might be involved, such as relocating children from one place to another, getting passports for children, how to deal with inheritances, pensions or interests in a business.

If you want to understand family law you need to understand not just the Matrimonial Causes Act (and the other pieces of legislation that affect family law) but also the court decisions that may be relevant to the issues involved in your case. That is why – unless your matter is very straightforward – you may need the help of a lawyer.

The law can be complex. To make it a bit more difficult, the most important laws are discretionary, which means that a Judge has a wide range of possibilities to choose from when determining arrangements for children or dividing up your property. There are no set formulas or rules to determine exactly what will be decided by the Judge, either for property distribution or for arrangements for the children. There are only broad guidelines within which the law operates.

Child support is also an important part of the broader family law. The child support system is designed to ensure that parents pay a reasonable amount for the care of their children after the breakdown of a relationship. The Child Support Agency was established to administer the system and distribute money from the paying parent to the receiving parent under formulas that have been modified over time.

'Fairness' and 'children's best interests'

"What you see and hear depends a good deal on where you are standing." – C.S. Lewis

'Fairness' and a 'child's best interests' are the fundamental principles on which the law is based. These are pretty broad concepts and are subject to widely differing interpretations.

There is generally no right and wrong in family law. There are just differing perceptions, views and shades of grey. Disputes tend to get exaggerated in the emotional environment of a breakup, so try to stand back from the conflict, be objective and aim to see things through the eyes of others as well as your own.

If you get caught up in the correctness of your position or on a principle of who is right and who is wrong, your experience with the legal process is likely to be a long and unsatisfying one.

It can sometimes seem that the legal system can only ever deliver a lose-lose result. You will always have less than you did before, because you are dividing up what was previously shared between you – whether it is your involvement with your children or the fruits of your financial endeavours.

Settling or going to court

The vast majority of people with family law issues do not want to get caught up in lengthy and expensive legal processes or in the courts. Most would prefer to get matters settled as quickly, inexpensively and amicably as is possible.

The legal process exists to help you do just that, by encouraging you to make voluntary agreements to finalise financial and children's issues, or by providing a forum for making decisions on issues you are unable to resolve with your ex-partner.

In most situations you will need to choose how you resolve your post-separation issues – either by going to court or by resolving them directly with your ex-partner. There are now several methods of 'Alternative Dispute Resolution' available, such as Mediation, Collaborative Law and Arbitration.

You can settle 'out of court' and the agreement can still be made legal and effective by obtaining approval of the same from the court. This can be done by just sending a financial (consent) order signed by the parties and a summary of the parties' financial position. This usually does not involve any court appearance, provided the court is satisfied that the agreement is fair and reasonable. However, if you can't get things resolved, you may have to take your dispute to the Family Courts and ask a Judge to rule on the issues.

If you have to go to court, you must follow the rules and regulations regarding court processes and procedures (these are dealt with in some detail in chapter 6 'If It positively, definitely has to go to court').

Even if you are already in the court process, you may still settle before the matter goes to a trial before a Judge. The vast majority of all cases that begin in the Family Courts are resolved before the Final Hearing, by agreement between the parties. If you do not resolve all of your issues, you may have to go to a Final Hearing to enable a Judge to examine the issues and make a decision that will then be binding on everyone.

Finalisation by agreement

Getting matters settled by agreement and without court action is almost always in your best interests.

Court cases can take over a year rather than months, so settlement will achieve substantial savings in both time and legal costs. A fair and reasonable settlement provides certainty and allows you to get on with your life without the unpredictable outcome of the court process. Settlement also reduces the potential for ongoing conflict between you and your ex (and the inevitable impact of parental conflict on children) and the potential involvement of your wider family and friends.

If you and your ex are able to agree on your property division or children's matters, you have several choices:

▶　　Children Matters - come to a private agreement with your ex-partner and follow through on it – whether you put it in writing or not.

▶　　Financial Matters for married couples - get a lawyer to draft up a Consent Order setting out your agreement and submit it to the court for approval, or

▶　　Financial Matters for unmarried couples - get a lawyer to prepare a Separation Deed.

If you want to resolve child support issues privately and without the intervention of the CMS, then any agreement reached in that respect can be included in the terms of a financial Consent Order (but only for married couples). If this is done, then it will prevent either of the parties to the agreement from taking the case to the CMS for the first 12 months from the date of the Order.

Resolution by the Courts

Sometimes matters ultimately have to go to court because:

- ▶ The parties simply cannot agree on proposals to resolve issues.

- ▶ There are substantial differences about the facts (or the interpretation of facts) or because your ex-partner is just 'not playing ball'.

- ▶ You are advised by your lawyer that it's in your interests to start the process to get the other party moving, or

- ▶ You may have an urgent need for the court to protect your children from harm or to preserve assets from being wasted or being sent outside the country.

Where agreement cannot be reached, you can make an application for the court to make decisions about property distribution and/or children's issues.

There are many and varied reasons that might justify starting legal proceedings. However, going to court should always be your last resort.

Court processes are explained in detail in chapter 6 'If it positively, definitely has to go to court'.

Divorce

Cohabiting couples do not need any court orders to confirm their separation or the end of their relationship. It is over when one or both decides that is the case.

Married couples however must apply to the court to obtain a divorce. If there has been an irretrievable breakdown of the marriage, as is required for every divorce case, then in order to divorce immediately, the person who wants to petition for the divorce must state that the other party has either committed adultery or that they have behaved unreasonably. If neither party wants to blame the other then the couple can wait until they have lived separately and apart for at least 2 years and they both agree to the divorce. If one does not agree, then the person who wants the divorce may have to wait until they have lived separately and apart for a minimum of 5 years, before they can divorce the other person, without needing their agreement. This is unusual however as you could cite their alleged unreasonable behaviour.

The rate of divorce in the UK has dropped steadily over the past ten years, apart from an increase in 2010. In 2011 there were 117,558 divorces. Research indicates that the number of marriage separations was highest in men and women aged 40 to 49. A significant number of people in this country live together as unmarried couples (cohabitees), but their breakups are not included in these statistics.

In the UK, it is now relatively easy to get a divorce. However, to do so, you must first prove that you were actually married. If you were married in the UK, this must have occurred in either a religious ceremony or a civil ceremony conducted by a person authorised by the government.

Are you married... or not?

Answering this question is not a problem for most people. A large percentage of our resident population were married in the UK. In many countries, a marriage is on record and it is easy to obtain documentary evidence from the registry where the marriage took place. Some countries can be slow at providing the documentation. In other countries, where there have been wars or natural disasters, the records may no longer be available. So, make sure that you start getting the documentation together as early as possible.

In some countries, there is no documentation and evidence of a marriage will have to be provided (usually by affidavits or statements from both parties) before a divorce can be granted. In brief, if you were validly married under the laws of the country where the marriage took place, the law of England and Wales generally accepts the validity of that marriage.

Annulment of a marriage

Annulment of a marriage is quite a different issue and is much more difficult to obtain than a divorce. A court will only make a declaration that a marriage is null and void in very limited circumstances. These include bigamous marriages or where the consent of a party to the marriage was obtained by fraud or duress.

It may be possible to claim that you were not married because of a mistake about the identity of the person you married.

However, you might have a better chance of getting an annulment if you did not understand 'the nature and consequences' of the ceremony you went through. Again, each case will depend on its own circumstances and the court may decide based on a wide range of factors whether or not, at the time you got married, you really understood what you were doing.

You may also be able to obtain an annulment if you were forced into a marriage against your will by threats or coercion.

Bigamy

Bigamy is the offence of marrying a person while already legally married to another person. If the first marriage is legal, the second is not. Under the Offences Against the Person Act 1861 a bigamist faces imprisonment for a term not exceeding 7 years (as well as the wrath of two people).

If you were married in a country where multiple marriages are legal, all marriages valid in that country would be recognised as legal in the UK and it is legal to bring all of your wives or husbands to the UK if you migrate.

Getting the divorce

There are very few contested divorces – where one party is opposed to the granting of the divorce. It takes two people to make a marriage but only one to break it.

To apply for a divorce, you must be in a position to prove all of the following:

▸ You are married (by providing a marriage certificate or other appropriate evidence of the relationship).

▸ That the marriage has irretrievably broken down.

▸ That either there has been adultery or unreasonable behaviour; a separation for 2 years and both parties agree to the divorce; desertion or that the couple have been separated for at least 5 years.

▸ That you satisfy the jurisdictional requirements.

If this is the case, you can file the relevant papers at court and, unless there are issues relating to the care of your children, you will get your divorce. In fact, you don't even need to attend court when the divorce is granted.

What is separation?

'Separation' is simply a state of fact that exists where one (or both) parties no longer consider themselves to be in a partnership and there is no reasonable prospect of reconciliation. You do not have to be living apart to be separated in the eyes of the law. You could be separated but still living 'under one roof', as long as the conditions for separation have occurred.

The court will require details regarding 'life under one roof' in order to get a divorce. The court will look to evidence of the end of the relationship and consider domestic arrangements – for example, who does the shopping, cooking, washing and cleaning. You may have an ongoing financial relationship and still be separated by law.

There is a 'kiss and make up' provision in the Matrimonial Causes Act that allows a separated couple to get back together for one single period or various combined periods up to a total of 6 months, to try and make the relationship work without affecting the date of their original separation.

Effectively, the 2 or 5 year separation period is suspended during the 'kiss and make up' period. Therefore, the period or periods of attempted reconciliation are not counted when calculating the 2 or 5-year separation period.

Have children under 18?

Before granting a divorce to a couple with children under the age of 18, the court must be satisfied that arrangements for the care of those children are appropriate.

A word about Wills

When you get married, any existing Will you may have made is automatically revoked. If this happens and you die without making a new Will, you will die intestate. Your estate may become the subject of a legal dispute between your relatives and those who think you should have made financial provision for them in your Will.

Decree Absolute upon divorce or a final Dissolution Order upon dissolution of a Civil Partnership, means that any provision for the former spouse/civil partner in any Will made following the marriage/civil partnership will cease to have effect.

Mediation

Under the Family Proceedings Rules, since April 2011, it was expected that all couples considering making a court application regarding either their finances or children, following a relationship breakdown, would be referred to Mediation. There are exemptions to this rule, but they are few and far between. Basically, the court will want evidence of the fact that all other possible avenues have been attempted to resolve matters before the court process is commenced.

From April 2014, it is due to become compulsory to attend a Mediation Information and Assessment Meeting (MIAM).

IT'S ALL ABOUT THE KIDS
– CHILDREN'S ISSUES

SUMMARY

The law when dealing with children matters and arrangements after separation is set out by the Children Act 1989. Its aim is to keep the law simple and child-centred.

You will probably have to compromise on arrangements for your children. Try to be flexible about the arrangements – it will be better for you and, more importantly, much better for your children. Compromise is the key.

Try to keep lines of communication open in the negotiation phase and after you have resolved children's issues. There are many decisions to be made about your children's future, and in almost all circumstances you will have to consult each other about them.

If your matters regarding your children end up with solicitors or in the court, try to keep a sense of proportion about what is happening – it's pointless spending £5,000 on legal bills for an argument over who should be washing and returning the children's school clothes when you could buy a second set for a fraction of the expense.

The way a court will see the children's situation may be quite different to the way you see it, or the way you would expect the court to see it.

Each child is an individual and, as they grow older, the court will pay more attention to their personalities and opinions. When making a decision about a child, a court will consider the child's wishes and feelings. The amount of weight attached to those wishes increases the older and more mature the child is.

If you want to move a long distance away from your partner, sharing time with your children will be difficult. These cases often wind up in court because it is difficult to decide whom the children should live with when the direct consequence is restricted contact with the other parent.

What does the law say?

A child is a person who is under 18 years of age, although the court will usually be slow to intervene in relation to children aged 16 or over, unless there is good reason. The overriding principle in children matters, and the court's primary consideration, is that the best interests and welfare of the child are paramount. The court will take into account several factors, collectively known as 'The Welfare Checklist' when making a decision on a Children Act application. These factors include the child's wishes and feelings, the care that each party is capable of giving to the child, whether there is any risk of harm to the child and what the likely effect will be on the child if there is a change in circumstances.

An important part of separating is to provide a framework to make proper arrangements for children after their parents separate. Court orders can be made which determine issues relating to children and almost any aspect of their upbringing. Such orders can cover specific arrangements for where the children are each minute of their lives, setting out who will be responsible for every aspect of their care and prescribing which schools, religious institutions and relatives they will be involved with (or not), where they are to be delivered and collected from when moving from one household to another, in what conveyance they are to travel and who (if anyone) is to supervise the handovers. They can also specify whether certain medication is to be administered, whom the children may telephone, when and at whose expense. In unusual cases, the orders can even specify what the children are to be fed and which clothes will travel with them (and in what condition), however it is unusual for a court to adjudicate on such matters, or to impose such strict conditions upon a responsible parent. It is important to remember that it is rarely in anyone's best interests to be tied down to such an extent, and the court would only do so in extreme circumstances and will be reluctant to make such an order.

Parents need to reach an agreement that resolves arrangements for the children in a way that respects their interests and promotes their welfare. If they don't, or can't do this, the courts will take an objective view as to what is best for the children, and impose such arrangements as it sees fit.

So, ask yourself:

▸ "Do the arrangements advance the best interests of our children – or not?"

All separated parents must deal with and resolve this fundamental question.

While it is not always possible for parents to agree fully on all aspects of a child's upbringing, most manage to reach a compromise they can live with – even though it might not be their number one preference. Remember that compromise and an element of flexibility are often essential in making arrangements for your children. It is usually essential to have an element of co-operation to make the arrangements work, and it is important to realise that reasonable flexibility will make everyone's life easier, and the day-to-day arrangements run more smoothly.

If you fight for every possible advantage and concede nothing, the conflict will go on and the stress levels will continue to rise. This will almost inevitably have a negative impact on the children. Compromise will help to reduce the levels of conflict and tension around children's issues. This in turn should make life very much easier for all, especially the children.

Some issues can never be compromised, such as the physical and emotional safety of your children. However, try to be as objective as possible. Keep in mind that the best interests of the children are what this is all about and that, sometimes, your own wishes on a particular issue may differ from those of the child. Pick your fights wisely and stand your ground only on really important issues.

The advantages of settling disputes without going to court apply to children's issues as they do to any other matters. Consider the cost, the time and the likely outcome and ask whether it's really worth going to court. Consider also the impact on the child of knowing that his/her parents are in court arguing about them. Exhaust your avenues for negotiation and dispute resolution before you commence proceedings.

What is Parental Responsibility (PR)?

As a parent you have obligations and responsibilities towards your children – not rights. The concept of Parental Responsibility was introduced by the Children Act 1989 and it is supposed to reaffirm this idea of obligations and responsibilities. The actual legal definition is "all the rights, duties, powers, responsibilities and authority which by law a parent of a child has in relation to the child and his property". It is important to remember that Parental Responsibility exists for the benefit of the child, not the parent.

In everyday life, the effect of PR is that anyone who has it has the right to obtain information about the child, such as medical updates and school reports, and the right to have a say in any important aspects of the child's upbringing. This includes decisions relating to education, religious upbringing, what the child's surname should be and whether or not he or she should have certain medical treatment.

Certain aspects of a child's upbringing, such as those listed above, must be agreed between everyone who has Parental Responsibility. Other more day-to-day decisions, such as what the child eats, or what activities they undertake whilst with a parent, do not necessarily need to be agreed. Parents often have different styles of parenting and provided they don't harm the child, they are unlikely to be criticised by a judge.

Who has Parental Responsibility (PR)?

Mothers automatically have PR when a child is born, however this is not the same for fathers. A father will have PR if:

▸ He was married to the mother either when the child was born, or subsequently.

▸ He is registered as the child's father on the birth certificate and the child was born after 1st December 2003.

▸ He has completed a Parental Responsibility Agreement with the mother, which has then been registered, or

▸ He has obtained a Residence or Parental Responsibility Order from the court (in the case of a Residence Order, Parental Responsibility only lasts for as long as the Residence Order remains in place).

It is possible for step-parents to obtain Parental Responsibility, but it is not always considered appropriate for them to do so. Step-Parents can obtain Parental Responsibility either by completing a Parental Responsibility Agreement with the mother (and with the father if he has PR) and then registering it, or by making an application to the court for an order.

Any other family members, for example grandparents, who obtain a Residence Order in regard to a child will also acquire Parental Responsibility, but it will only last for as long as the Residence Order remains in place.

Arrangements for the children and how to resolve issues of their upbringing

Getting it resolved by agreement

It is always advisable for parents to work together after they have separated in order to work out the arrangements for bringing up their children. It can be an unsettling time for any child and their best interests must be at the forefront of any decision made. When discussing arrangements for their children, parents should place a large notice in front of them that reads:

THE DECISIONS WE MAKE ARE IN THE BEST INTERESTS OF OUR CHILDREN

Do not allow the children to become 'collateral damage' to the emotional fallout of your separation. They are not responsible for the split and parents have a responsibility to minimise any suffering they experience as a result of it. It is important to remember that your relationship as a couple (however damaged it may be) is separate to your relationship as parents. As difficult as it is, you must separate out your animosity on a personal level towards the other person when making important decisions about the children. You also need to remember that your views about the children's best interests are very important, but they are only one person's view.

Don't start with an extreme position that is not sustainable, or pretend to seek conditions that you are really willing to sacrifice in exchange for others. To do so is only playing with your children's welfare and will rarely gain any favour with an objective observer, such as a judge. That kind of approach just puts your interests before those of your children and the 'game' is not likely to be successful. The other parent will likely respond to the tactic by taking a totally opposite position and you will end up too far apart for meaningful negotiations to take place.

It is worthwhile thinking about what your worst-case scenario might be. For example, consider how little time the kids might end up spending with you if the matter goes to court and it all goes wrong.

If you think that is pretty bleak, the scenario could become even bleaker if you engage in a court battle over children's issues. The more you fight, the less chance you will have of getting the matter resolved as you might wish – and the more expense you will incur. The final decisions will be made by a judge who (correctly) will take only the needs of the children into consideration, not yours. The judge's decision may not be what you want.

What should parents consider?

Minimising any negative impact of moving between two parents in different homes at different times is extremely important. Therefore, if parents can decide on a mutual approach to bringing up the children, everyone will benefit. Decisions parents will have to make include:

- Where the children will live (one place or two?).

- What religious celebrations and worship the children will take part in.

- What type of education and schools the children should attend.

- What attendance at sporting and extra-curricular activities is appropriate.

- How to fit in with the parents' work arrangements.

- When and where the children should spend time with others (grandparents and other relatives).

- What the handover arrangements will be.

- How to make arrangements for the children during holidays (school holidays and long weekends).

- What arrangements should be in place for birthdays, special and family celebrations.

- Whether the children have any special needs, including medical requirements, and how these will be catered for.

- What arrangements are reasonable for spending time with siblings and step siblings, and

- How to bring flexibility into the terms of the agreement to provide for future events.

If you are having difficulties making these arrangements with your ex-partner then you can consider Mediation, where an independent third party will help you both reach an agreement. Alternatively, you could instruct a solicitor to put forward your proposals in writing. There are also collaboratively trained solicitors, who will facilitate a 'round-table meeting' whereby both parents, with the help of their solicitors, try and work out an agreed solution to any child care issues. It must be noted that Mediators will not give legal advice; only solicitors are able to do that.

If an agreement cannot be reached, the last resort would be to issue court proceedings. However, if you are planning to fight over your children in the court, stop and think, "Why am I doing this? What do I stand to achieve?" Perhaps you will decide that it is time to discuss the issues with your ex and negotiate a solution.

Getting it resolved by the court

In most cases, you are expected to attend a Mediation Information Assessment Meeting (MIAM) before any court application is issued. This is an initial meeting with a Mediator to discuss your options and whether Mediation would be the better option to try and resolve the issues or not. If Mediation is not the better option, then the Mediator will complete a form to enable you to issue court proceedings with. There are certain circumstances in which you are not expected to attend a MIAM, such as when there is an emergency, if the children are at risk of imminent harm, or if there has been domestic abuse.

What type of orders can the court make?

The four most common orders the court makes in relation to children are:

- ▶ Residence/Shared Residence Orders.

- ▶ Contact Orders.

- ▶ Specific Issue Orders.

- ▶ Prohibited Steps Orders.

These are collectively known as Section 8 Orders and usually last until the child reaches the age of 18.

It is important to remember that the court can make whichever orders it believes are necessary to protect the interests of the child. This means that if you apply for any one of the above orders, there is no guarantee either that the other parent will not apply for a different order, or that the court will not make one of the other types of orders, if the circumstances of the case require it.

It is also important to take into account that the court can refuse to make any orders at all. Under the Children Act 1989, there is a 'No Order' presumption, which the court applies to all cases. This means that the court will not make an order unless it is absolutely necessary and it would be of positive benefit to the child to do so.

Many people still refer to 'custody' and 'access'. Custody had greater rights attached to it, and was therefore often seen as the 'winning' order, and a 'prize' for being the better parent. Sadly, some parents showed little interest in having regular access if they did not 'win' custody. The Children Act 1989 fundamentally changed the principle and words used in relation to children as follows:

- ▸   'Custody' became 'Parental Responsibility'

- ▸   'Care and control' became 'residence'.

- ▸   'Access' became 'contact'.

Despite the changes in language, the core principle has remained the same: "the best interests of the child should be the determining factor in deciding how a child's time should be divided as between his or her parents."

Residence/ Shared Residence Orders

A Residence Order sets out with which parent a child will live. The court can also make Shared Residence Orders that provides for the child to live with both parents in their respective households. Such orders usually set out exactly how the child's time will be divided between the two parents/households. A Shared Residence Order can be useful in reassuring a child they are being cared for by both parents, and can also be a useful tool for reminding parents that they remain equal in the eyes of the law, and neither has more control over the child than the other. A Shared Residence Order does not necessary mean that the children will spend equal time with both parents. Such an order can however reflect the importance of both parents in the children's lives.

Contact Orders

The court's position in relation to contact is that it is the child's right to have a relationship with both their parents, rather than the other way round. Therefore, the starting point is that the child should have contact with both parents, unless it can be demonstrated that contact would adversely affect the child's welfare.
A Contact Order requires the parent with whom the child lives to make the child available for contact with the other parent on the dates and times set out in the order. This can include direct contact (face-to-face), such as overnight contact and visiting contact and/or indirect contact (via letter, telephone, email or Skype).

Contact Orders can be expressed in general terms or strictly defined to include the exact days and times when it is to take place. They can include the arrangements for collection and return of the child, and can also contain set conditions, for example specifying the location at which contact will take place.

Most Contacts Orders also have Warning Notices attached, which warn the parent with whom the child lives that if they do not abide by the terms of the contact order, various enforcement provisions can apply. These provisions include unpaid work (like community service), fines and even imprisonment.

Specific Issue Orders

Specific Issues Orders deal with a specific issue arising in regard to a child's upbringing. Examples can include: which school the child should attend, whether they should have a certain operation or vaccination, what religion they should adopt and whether they should go away on holiday. A Specific Issue Order will be worded so as to grant permission to either parent to undertake the specified course of action, even if the other parent does not agree.

Prohibited Steps Orders

Prohibited Steps Orders also deal with specific issues, but instead of granting permission, they prevent the person named in the order from taking a particular course of action in respect of the child. This can include orders preventing the parent from changing the child's name or school, from undertaking religious rites (e.g. circumcision or christening), or from removing the child from England and Wales.

What does the court take into consideration when they make an order?

When the court deals with any application they will always have the child's welfare as their paramount consideration. They will also be wary about any delay, as it is generally considered that prolonged uncertainty can be damaging to all concerned, especially the children. It is however good to remember that it can be useful to review the arrangements at appropriate intervals to check they are still working for everyone.

When considering a child's welfare, the court will consider the factors set out below, which are collectively known as the Welfare Checklist. These factors can also be a useful checklist when you are preparing your application and when you present your case to the Judge:

- Wishes and feelings of the child (taking into account their age, level of understanding and maturity).

- The child's physical, emotional and educational needs.

- The likely effect that any change of circumstances will have on the child.

- The child's age, sex, background and any characteristics that the court thinks are relevant.

- Any harm that the child may have suffered or is at risk of suffering;

- How capable the parties in the case are of meeting the child's needs (emotional and physical).

- All of the powers that the court has under the Children Act which could be used within the proceedings.

Attempting to influence the children

The courts take a very dim view of anyone who tries to influence a child against either of their parents, or other members of the family. The courts will always expect parents not to discuss any disputed issues or belittle each other in the presence of the children.

You may hold genuine views about the behaviour of the other parent, but communicating these views to the children, trying to get them to agree, or generally trying to influence their attitude towards the other parents is unlikely to help.

Quite aside from the negative impact it can have on your case before the court, it is also considered to be very damaging to a child, both in the short and long term. It is therefore important to consider the children's interests not only when you are considering what the arrangements for them should be, but also when you think about how this is going to be communicated to them.

CAFCASS – Child and Family Court Advisory and Support Service

CAFCASS act as an independent advisor to the court. Whether or not they have an ongoing role in the proceedings depends on the issues in the case.

When an application is made to court under the Children Act, CAFCASS will undertake background searches in relation to the family, known as Safeguarding Checks. These checks include information from the police and social services, to see whether there are any records in regards to anyone involved in the proceedings. Any information is then sent to the court prior to the first hearing, in order to help the court decide whether there are welfare issues that need to be addressed in the proceedings.

In most cases, a duty CAFCASS officer will be present at the first hearing (known as a 'Conciliation Appointment'). They will usually listen to what both parents are saying, consider the background to the case and help everyone, including the judge, to define what the issues in dispute are, and whether it would assist the court for CAFCASS to prepare a report.

Only the judge, in consultation with CAFCASS, can decide whether or not CAFCASS should prepare a report for the proceedings, and whilst both parents will be given the chance to express their views on whether such a report would be useful, it is not possible for a parent (or anyone else who is a party to the proceedings) to insist on or refuse a report. In most court proceedings the judge may take the view that the issues can be resolved without the need for a CAFCASS report.

CAFCASS Reports usually focus on two main issues: the wishes and feelings of the children (if they are of an age where this is appropriate) and any welfare concerns that have been raised in the proceedings. The CAFCASS Officer will consider court papers such as applications and witness statements, speak to the parents, and to the children, and if appropriate and/or necessary, the child's school or doctor, as well as other members of the family.

They will then make a recommendation as to the best outcome in regard to the matter in dispute, taking into account all of this information. The recommendation in a CAFCASS Report is given considerable weight by the court, and it is usually very difficult to persuade a judge that they should not follow that recommendation when making any final decision.

If a case proceeds all the way to a Final Hearing, the CAFCASS Report will form an important part of the evidence before the Judge. Often, the CAFCASS Officer will attend the Final Hearing in order to answer any questions on their report or about what they have recommended and why.

When considering whether or not a CAFCASS Report is likely to be useful in any given case, it is important to recognise the effect they have on the timescale for reaching a final decision. It is not uncommon for a CAFCASS Report to take 3-4 months to prepare, so it is advisable to raise the possibility of one being done at the first possible opportunity if you think it would help the case.

Appointment of a Guardian

If the issues in the case are particularly complicated, or if the child is of an age where their wishes and feelings will be a very important factor in the final decision, the child can be made a party to the court proceedings. This is done by the appointment of a Guardian for the proceedings. The Guardian is usually a CAFCASS Officer or similar professional. They will then work with a Solicitor to present the child's case to the court.

The appointment of a Guardian can only be made with the authorisation of the court. It is another way in which the court can get a separate view on the issues in dispute which is independent of the parents' own wishes.

When it's resolved – complying with court orders

Once a court order is made, whether it was by agreement or following the decision of the judge, both parents are expected to comply with it unless there are exceptional circumstances.

The circumstances in which a court will consider it justifiable not to comply with an order will be very limited, and you will generally be expected to show that it was impossible for you to comply with the order, or that you had a genuine concern that the child would be placed at risk if you complied with it.

If you fail to comply with the terms of an order without sufficient justification, you will be considered to have breached the order, which is Contempt of Court. The court can then apply a sanction, including:

▸ Payment of a fine.

▸ Unpaid community work.

For more serious or repeated breaches, the court can send a parent to prison, or order a change of residence to the other parent.

Given the seriousness with which the breach of an order is considered by the court, it is strongly recommended that you take legal advice if you do not wish to follow the terms of an order.

The following are useful points to bear in mind when separating and when dealing with child care arrangements:

Criticising the other parent (or their family)

A parent should not attempt to influence the children against the other parent or the other parent's family. Neither parent should use their children as pawns in battles over the spoils of a relationship that has ended, or to inflict damage on the other. It is worth repeating: a parent does not stop being a parent simply because of separation.

Attitude towards responsibilities as a parent and towards the other

The attitude each parent shows (and has shown in the past) towards their responsibilities as a parent is an important factor in deciding what arrangements should be put in place for children.

While this may sound obvious, remember that when decisions are made about where the children will live, a parent who has demonstrated and continues to demonstrate a positive interest in the welfare of the children, and the ability to foster a positive image of the other parent, will be better placed than a parent who has not. That is not to suggest this is a competition to decide which parent has the 'best attitude'. Both parents can be positive and properly concerned about the children's welfare and demonstrate this through their actions. Equally, a parent who simply talks about how interested they are in their children's welfare but does little by way of practical activity will find it hard to convince a court that their proposals for the children are the best.

Another consideration is how each parent has promoted the relationship of the children with the other parent. If you prevent the children from having contact with the other parent, or make negative comments to them about the other parent, out of dislike or blame for the breakdown of the relationship, this is unlikely to advance your cause, and can have serious consequences, including limitations being placed upon contact to prevent the child from distress caused by such behaviour.

The age and stage of the children

Arrangements for the children will need to take into account their ages, their relationships with each other and their routine. Arrangements will usually need to be reconsidered at various stages as the children grow up, or as circumstances change.

Social research has shown that as a general rule, a younger child needs shorter but more frequent periods with the 'non-primary' parent. As a child gets older, the periods can successfully be longer, but less frequent. There is however no hard and fast rule, and it is important to tailor the arrangements to the circumstances of your individual family.

The wishes of the child are relevant to what is in their best interests, and become an increasingly important factor in the decision. The courts are less likely to intervene and make any orders the older a child gets. It is generally only in unusual circumstances that the court will make an order once a child has reached the age of 16. There is no set rule about the age at which a child's views carry greater weight, and this usually depends on their level of understanding and maturity, as considered against the complexity of the situation and the decision to be made.

Education, religion and cultural issues

Schooling, religion and social and cultural backgrounds may be important considerations when negotiating arrangements for children. The issues will be different in every case and should be thought through carefully before any orders are sought from the court.

Given the complexity of this area of law and the potential consequences of making the wrong decision legally, it is always advisable to obtain legal advice as soon as possible. If you are the parent whose child has been abducted, you may be entitled to legal aid for any proceedings that are needed to secure your child's return.

Whilst there are many international arrangements in place to try and secure the return of an abducted child, some countries are not signed up to these agreements, and some that are do not have good systems in place to make this happen. It is never advisable to rely on using these agreements, and prevention is always better than the cure. Consider obtaining orders from the court and/or taking special measures around the arrangements for contact. You can also ask the Passport Agency not to issue passports for the children (although sometimes you will need an order for this) and it is advisable to keep a copy of the child's passport details and their pictures, as this will all help if the worst happens. If your children are abducted, it is wise to see a solicitor as soon as possible, as it is usually easier to issue a successful application if you have acted quickly.

Passports

Children's passports are often an issue, involving arguments as to whether or not the child should have a passport and, if so, which parent should look after that passport when it is not in use.

It is important to remember that a child may be entitled to a passport from more than one country. If you and your ex-partner cannot agree on whether or not a child should have a passport, or from which country they should have one, you can make an application to the court for the court to determine the issue. If a parent refuses to agree to the issuing of a passport in circumstances where the court believes one should be obtained, the court can order the parent to sign the application and, in default, can execute the documents on behalf of that parent if they still will not do so.

If there are concerns that the other parent may obtain a passport in secret, without agreement, it is advisable to write to the Passport Agency to ask them not to issue any passports for the child. This request should also be sent to the relevant authority of any other country from which the child is entitled to travel documents. The court can also make an order prohibiting the issue of a passport.

There is no law on which of the parents should look after the child's passport once it has been issued. Many judges will suggest that the parent with whom the child lives on a day-to-day basis should hold the passport, but it will always depend on the facts of the individual case. In some circumstances, the court can order that the travel documents are surrendered to a solicitor or to the court and only released to either parent with the authority of the court.

DIVIDING UP THE PROPERTY ON DIVORCE – WHO GETS WHAT, AND WHEN

SUMMARY

▸ 'Financial Matters' in family law are the issues involved in the division of your assets, income and liabilities after separation. They were formerly referred to as 'Ancillary Relief'.

▸ 'Property' includes many things – it is not just cash and houses. If you have a family business, a trust, investments, an entitlement to be paid, or a pension entitlement, it is likely to be defined as property.

▸ Property also includes money you owe and any other liabilities of the relationship.

▸ All property will be included for consideration in the financial distribution after separation. However, some property may be ring fenced in certain circumstances – this is a potentially complex area, so best to consult a lawyer before deciding what should and what shouldn't be included in the marital pot.

▸ Make sure you have a Final Order that is approved by the court setting out how you have divided your property. If you don't and your ex later wants another slice of the property, you could be in for a nasty surprise.

▸ One party's contribution is unlikely to have any effect on the overall settlement – so if one of you were the breadwinner and the other the homemaker, your contributions would be considered equal.

▸ What each of you is likely to need in the future will also be taken into account.

▸ It is very important that you tell the truth about what you own, to each other and to the court. This is called "full and frank disclosure". If you don't, you could end up transferring a lot more to your ex than you thought you might save by not disclosing all the information.

> ▸ Don't go off and spend money, dispose of or destroy property to try to minimise the amount your ex will get. This is likely to backfire and may be deducted from the property that you receive in the distribution.

> ▸ Pensions are included in property distribution, but are not necessarily treated in the same way as other property.

What is 'property'?

When a couple separates, they will have to decide how their property will be divided between them (and how they will repay any debts).

In everyday language, 'property' means virtually anything – whether it is an asset or a liability (debt of some kind).

'Property' does not just include real estate (e.g. homes, farms, apartments, office blocks, land). It may also include:

> ▸ Personal items (furniture, kitchenware, white goods).

> ▸ Money (cash, bank accounts).

> ▸ Debts owed to you or by you (to the bank as mortgages or personal loans, credit cards, loans from or to friends or business associates).

> ▸ Investments (shares, interests in a business or company, timeshares).

> ▸ A family business.

> ▸ A trust.

> ▸ An entitlement to be paid or a liability to pay in the event that something happens.

> ▸ Intellectual property.

> ▸ Lottery winnings, and

> ▸ Gifts from parents and relatives and, in some circumstances, inheritances.

'Property' even includes entitlements to redundancy or long service payments, leave entitlements, pensions and superannuation.

Whatever financial items you can think of, it is almost certainly 'property' in the family law sense. That means all of the property – whether it's in your name, your partner's name, joint names, a company you may have an interest in, or even property in someone else's name that you have some entitlement to. In effect...

WHAT'S YOURS IS OURS, WHAT'S MINE IS OURS AND WHAT'S OURS IS OURS.

It's all in the pot and available for distribution between yourselves, even if one party has never shown any interest in it, did not want it or tried to get rid of it. If it's still there, it's included in the pot. And if it's not property, it will usually be regarded as a 'financial resource' (more on that later).

Sometimes, especially in a short relationship where there are no children, dividing up the property can be pretty easy as there is often not much to split between you. However, even in these cases, you still need an order drafted up and lodged at court (be aware that if you don't, it may come back to bite you).

It can get to be quite complicated where a lot of property has been accumulated over the years or where there are complex financial arrangements and structures. Whatever your circumstances you will almost certainly need some good legal advice and a final court order setting out exactly who gets what.

Whether easy or complicated, always remember that the arrangements you make with your ex-partner will not be legally binding (that is, you cannot make the other party abide by the agreement) unless it is included within a Final Order approved by the court.

You can settle your property distribution by mutual agreement or you can go to court to ask for a decision from a Judge. The principles that should guide you in arriving at a private settlement and the law that the court will use are the same.

How do you determine who gets what, and when?

Lawyers are often criticised for complicating the law and making it almost impossible to understand. We are going to do the opposite – even at the risk of being accused of simplicity – and explain the principles of property or financial distribution in a very straightforward way.

Step 1 – Assess the assets and liabilities

Every item of property has a value and, if in doubt, there is always someone who will be able to provide a professional valuation. This could be an estate agent for your house, an actuary for any pensions, a forensic accountant for the business, etc.

The judge is interested only in the net monetary value of property. Sentimental value is not relevant (although it may be material to how you personally 'value' a particular item of property). You may regard Granny's necklace as priceless but an expert will put a monetary value on it.

In terms of endowments or investments, the court won't look at the projected or future value, but rather the current realisable value, i.e. if you were to cash it in today.

ASSET AND LIABILITY CALCULATIONS

A good way to tackle negotiations for financial distribution is to prepare a spreadsheet that includes all of the assets and liabilities.

This gives you a good picture of where you stand and also identifies what assets and liabilities have to be included in any agreement or orders (if you leave something out you may end up back in court to tie up the loose ends).

A schedule like this also enables you to work out the percentage of the assets you will get.

Put the assets and liabilities into columns and see what each totals. Then take the total liabilities away from the total assets. The result is the net value of the asset pool. In the example that follows, we have set out the assets and the liabilities. Subtract the liabilities from the assets to get the net asset figure £610,000, when you add up the three columns.

Note that the figures for the pension £150,000 and £80,000 are detailed separately and not added to the net available assets (we will explain later why it is best to keep pensions separate).

We have also included a column showing who owns each item of property – as 'mine' and 'yours'. This will help when you have to work out transfers of property that might have to take place.

Example of how you can set out what is in your marital pot

	Joint	*Mine*	*Yours*
House £650,000 Mortgage £200,000 Cost of Sale £15,000	£435,000		
Investment property		£50,000	
Savings/Policies	£100,000	£25,000	£50,000
Cars		£10,000	£30,000
Liabilities	(£150,000)	(£15,000)	(£25,000)
Net available assets	**£485,000**	**£70,000**	**£55,000**
Pensions		£150,000	£80,000
Income Salary p.m. net Benefits (e.g. tax credits/child benefit) Child Maintenance		£5,000 (£1,000)	£2,000 £120 £1,000
Total Income		£4,000	£3,120

When do you value the assets and liabilities?

The value of your assets and liabilities will be made at the date the property is divided between you.

If the matter goes to court, the value will be what things are worth at the time of the hearing.

If you are settling matters between yourselves, there is more flexibility as to the value. You may agree the values between yourselves, but they should still reflect approximate values at the date of your agreement.

How do you value the property?

If you cannot agree on values and are going to court, experts will have to be engaged. This can be a costly exercise, especially if you have businesses to value. Even valuations of homes may involve a jointly appointed valuer. These costs are significant. An argument over jewellery, antiques or other valuables might also involve professional valuers. However, it's rarely worth getting a valuation of your household contents as second hand furniture has a notoriously low value – you're both going to have to buy new items, so split the contents fairly between you both and don't involve solicitors as it can often cost you more in legal fees than what the items are actually worth.

Obtain several valuations from estate agents for your property (these are free) and agree to take an average of, say, three. If you do request letters from estate agents, ask them to put in writing their opinion as to the price at which they believe the property will sell (known as the 'open market value') as opposed to the price at which they recommend the property should be marketed for sale. That is usually much higher.

Get your accountant to place a value on your business interests and see if you can agree on that too. Try splitting your personal effects and furniture by mutual agreement. There are several ways of achieving a fair split without getting expensive valuations done. Compromise is the key.

In some cases, it will not be possible to agree on values, especially where the stakes are high and the consequences of the distribution may be unfair to one party – for example, where the separating couple own a business that one of them will keep after the distribution of property. The business may have provided the sole source of income for the parties during their relationship and, therefore, its value will be very important for the party who is not keeping that interest. A professional valuation by an agreed valuer may be the only way to produce a fair result and, in such cases, the parties will simply have to wear the costs and move on – ideally as quickly as possible, as protracted arguments over values are rarely of benefit to anyone but the professionals who charge fees for preparing the valuation reports.

Beware of values that may be volatile or change quickly, such as the price of shares and other financial investments. Make sure that the value you are agreeing to is the value at the date of implementation of your agreement, or you may find yourself short-changed.

The value you place on bank accounts and credit cards is also a potential trap. Make sure you are very clear about what is included and what is not. For example:

▸ Is a tax refund coming in soon? How much is it likely to be and who is entitled to it?

▸ Is one party cranking up a credit card bill that the other has to pay?

Just make sure the rules are agreed between you, as this leaves far less possibility for argument further down the track.

WHAT IS IT WORTH?

The task of valuing assets can often be simple – but this is not always the case.

The family home and real estate

Often it will be sufficient to obtain a written valuation from a local estate agent (an appraisal) at no cost. Remember, this may be higher than what the property will actually sell for. This is because an estate agent will give a figure that the property should be placed on the market for – sometimes to test the market – rather than their opinion as to what the property is actually likely to sell for. For this figure you either have to actually sell the property and let the market find its true value, or instruct a valuer to provide their opinion as to the amount you are likely to sell your property for.

So where there is no agreement about the value, it will be necessary to engage a professional valuer to conduct an inspection and write a report. This is usually done on behalf of both parties and, in most cases, the parties will share the cost of the report equally. The cost will depend on the size, nature and value of the property and is generally between £200 and £700 plus VAT.

Vehicles
In most cases, it will be enough to provide an estimate of value, or an internet print out from a car sales website such as the What Car Guide. Vintage and luxury cars are an exception. Remember to make an allowance for any loans taken out to purchase the car.

Furniture, artwork and jewellery
Furniture and other belongings are often not valued because, in most cases, the resale value is extremely low, and only a fraction of replacement value.

The most common approach is to estimate the value of this property or to disregard it altogether.

If furniture and belongings are an important part of your settlement, we would suggest preparing a list of items you would like to keep so that these matters can be raised and agreed early in the negotiations.

Of course, if there are expensive items, such as artwork or antique furniture, it may be worthwhile to have these items valued.

Jewellery is not always valued unless there are especially valuable pieces and will usually be kept by the person in possession. Generally, engagement and wedding rings will not form part of a property pool and will be kept by the wearer.

Companies, businesses and trusts
Valuing companies, business and trust assets can be a difficult task and experts will often have to be engaged to provide a valuation. Experts should be asked not only to value the business, but also address issues of liquidity and sustainable future income.

If it is clear that a business or a company is not very profitable, it may not be cost effective to obtain a valuation.

The valuation of these types of assets or resources requires ongoing cooperation by both parties. If you are not willing to cooperate, it can be expensive to obtain a valuation or to identify whether the company or business is even profitable.

Step 2 – Do any assets fall outside the marital pot?

Having worked out what is in the pool of assets and placed a value on each asset and debt, there may be assets that fall outside the marital pot. These would potentially include an inheritance received by one party or pre-acquired wealth (i.e. capital that one party had acquired before marriage). Basically, any money not made through the joint venture of the couple may fall outside the marital pot.

Whether you will actually be successful in excluding a particular asset, for example an inheritance, from the marital pot depends on several factors, such as: when during the marriage was it received? How much was it? How had the parties viewed it? Is it needed to help house one party and/or the children? So, for example, if one party inherited £100,000 six months before the parties separated, always kept it separate from the marital assets and there was sufficient other capital to meet the capital needs of the other party, then you have a much stronger chance of ring-fencing the money (i.e. keeping it for yourself) than if you received £5,000 in the first few years of a long marriage. Another way of looking at it is to ask whether there is sufficient money to meet both parties' needs without having to dip into the inheritance money. If the answer is yes, you have a much better chance of keeping the capital out of the marital pot.

What about contributions?

Contributions during the marriage unless exceptional, will generally not be considered. So if one party goes out to work and makes all the money, their contribution is valued as the same as the party who stayed at home to either look after the children or carry out domestic duties generally. In family law both parties' contributions are considered equal regardless of what they were.

Contributions prior to the relationship

Contributions to the asset pool are not restricted to what happened during the relationship. A contribution will be taken into account if it was made prior to when the relationship began or after the couple separated.

Contributions made prior to the relationship can be important, especially in shorter relationships. For example, if the marital pot in a four-year childless relationship is £500,000, and £300,000 was brought in by one party at the beginning, that person will have made a substantially greater contribution to the marital pot. This would then entitle them to a greater share of the assets pool when it is divided up. Current case law indicates that the court will try to assess the position of the parties prior to the marriage, then divide what was made during the marriage equally between them both – so in this case the party who brought the £300,000 to the marriage would retain it, plus a further £100,000 for their half of the balance.

Step 3 – What do each of the parties need in terms of capital and income, otherwise known as the Section 25 Factors.

The factors to be taken into account when dividing up the marital pot are set out in Section 25 of the Matrimonial Causes Act 1973. They take into account each party's situation and include the following:

- Both parties' age and health.

- Income, including earning capacity.

- Financial resources, which includes available assets, property, savings and pension provision.

- The standard of living enjoyed during the marriage.

- Any relevant contributions, although the scope for arguments in respect of contributions tends to be limited as indicated above.

- How long you lived together

It also includes:

- "To have regard to all the circumstances of the case."

In simple language, this last factor means that the law permits a Judge to take into account virtually anything. In practice, however, the courts have been quite restrictive about what they are prepared to take into account. For example, they do not consider a party's moral behaviour to be material to the financial outcome.

Violence by one party against another is generally regarded as relevant to financial distribution only in extreme cases, say if the violence has an impact on the other person's contributions, for example, by making it impossible for a party to work.

Examples of factors that may be considered relevant include:

▸ If you have been at home looking after the children for many years and you have little prospect of getting a properly paid job. Here a financial adjustment would probably be made to offset the fact that you may struggle to re-enter the workforce and have no capacity to support yourself as a result of your responsibilities for the children during, and after, the relationship.

▸ If one of you is elderly (beyond working age) and/or has health problems, while the other is in good health (and, therefore, has a greater capacity to work and support themselves), an adjustment may be made in favour of the less able person.

▸ If you have not worked for some time but intend to undertake a training course or studies that would help you to re-enter the workforce, an adjustment might be made (or spousal maintenance paid) to assist in this regard.

▸ If you are still responsible for the care and welfare of your children and you wish to continue that role, it may be necessary for an adjustment to be made to support that.

▸ If you are living with a new partner or plan to re-marry, then your new partner's finances could be taken into account as a 'financial resource'.

▸ If you are approaching retirement age, then the court will be particularly interested in your financial position post-retirement and the adjustments that may need to be made to the standard of living enjoyed.

At the end of the day, each case will depend entirely on its own facts and it would be wise to get legal advice about how adjustments might work in your particular situation.

Length of the relationship

How long parties have lived together is important. The longer you have been together, the more likely it is that your assets will be more equally shared after separation (and the less important the initial contributions will be considered to be, even if they were substantial).

The length of a relationship is taken from the time the parties start living together in a domestic relationship ('cohabitation'). If you are married, the beginning of your relationship will not necessarily be the date of your marriage; it will start from when you began to live together. This can be a significant factor when parties have lived together for a long time before getting married. The whole of their time together is taken to assess the length of the relationship.

A word about 'spousal maintenance'

'Spousal maintenance' (also known as 'periodical payments') is the financial support one party provides to the other after the relationship has ended. Maintenance may be payable for a short period of time or may be payable indefinitely. Either way, it is generally paid every month, is sometimes index linked and can be terminated at a fixed time in the future, e.g. when the youngest child is no longer dependent (known as "term maintenance") or it can be paid on a "joint lives basis", i.e. until either party dies, or until the payee remarries.

Generally, spousal maintenance is payable where:

▸ One party has a need for financial support.

▸ The other party has the capacity to provide that support, and

▸ It would be proper in all the circumstances that the support be provided, e.g. where there is a significant disparity in the parties' incomes.

Typically, this would occur where one person is the income earner and the other has inadequate means of support as a consequence of the separation. On-going periodical payments may be required if there are insufficient assets to distribute, which would give the needy party some other means of support.

Spousal maintenance can be paid under a court order or by agreement between the parties.

Sometimes spousal maintenance is capitalised, by way of a lump sum or an allowance of the percentage distribution as a substitute for on-going regular payments. This can be done by nominating a lump sum amount in a settlement and/or in orders, or by adjusting the percentage distribution.

You should seek legal advice if you are on either side of the spousal maintenance equation. This will give you some pointers about entitlements or obligations and about the proper way to give legal effect to lump sum payments.

Spousal maintenance is one of the most complicated, uncertain and emotive issues in many divorces. There is a wide range of possible outcomes regarding the level at which spousal maintenance should be paid and the term over which it should be paid.

Family Law – a discretionary jurisdiction

Remember, the law is discretionary and judges have a broad range within which they make their final decisions. No one can predict exactly what the result will be. Lawyers can only give you a range within which the matter is likely to be decided – something like "you should expect to receive somewhere between 60 per cent and 70 per cent of the net assets" or "your best case is £x and your worst case scenario is £y". So, if you launch into court proceedings to resolve your property dispute, make sure that what you are seeking is well within the probable range.

When assessing what you might end up with from a property settlement, don't forget to take into account your possible legal fees.

You may be spending a lot of money on legal fees for the privilege of having your dispute dealt with by the courts. For example, if you are 5 per cent apart overall and your lawyer tells you that your legal fees are likely to be around £25,000, the money you spend on those fees may be more than the percentage difference you are arguing about. In other words, if you are arguing over 5 per cent and the legal fees might be £25,000, your total net property would have to be worth well over £500,000 to make the argument worthwhile.

Always make this calculation in your decision-making process, whether the legal fees are fixed by your lawyer or estimates of what it might cost (in which case, take the top end of the estimate).

The benefits of trying to get matters resolved by agreement and staying out of the courts – as well as the value of compromise – are obvious.

Disclosure of financial information

An issue that often causes problems in property matters is full and frank disclosure of all the relevant financial information. Failure to provide adequate information is a significant reason why many cases end up going to court, rather than getting settled.

In family law, you have a duty to make a full and frank disclosure of your financial position to your ex-partner. This includes not just bank statements and title deeds but any information that is even remotely relevant to your financial position, including any interest in trusts, companies and also any interest or involvement in anything that is not even in your name.

The courts are very strict in their interpretation of this duty. Have a look at the Form E Financial Statement that everyone who goes to court has to complete, whether they are on Income Support or the CEO of a multi-national company. This document will tell you exactly what you must disclose and what supporting documents you must exhibit to your Form E Financial Statement.

In many relationships, one partner handles the major financial transactions while the other manages money for shopping, personal spending and day-to-day costs. In these situations the 'non-finance' partner often knows very little about the property of the parties: who owns what, where the money is coming from, what are the debts and how they are being paid off. This is a pretty common arrangement in many families today.

The situation provides an opportunity for one person to hide, or simply fail to disclose all of the assets when the discussion gets around to the financial settlement after separation. It also leaves one of the parties vulnerable to liabilities or debts that they were entirely unaware of.

The court has taken a consistently tough line on the obligation to make a full and frank disclosure of all assets, liabilities and other financial resources. In fact, if you are asking the court to make any kind of property orders, you must state that you have made a full disclosure in the documents that you file in the court.

Additionally, the court has powers to enforce disclosure – including the power to compel production of documents (anything that has been 'published', e.g. paper, soft-copy, electronic, etc.). It can even issue an order that enables the compulsory seizure of documents to ensure they are preserved. Orders can be made against third parties, such as banks, financial institutions, employers, trustees and the like, requiring them to produce relevant financial information. Virtually any document

relating to an asset can be requested and it must be produced for disclosure.
If a person fails to produce financial information in accordance with the court timetable – for example, they do not produce their Form E Financial Statement on time – then it is possible to apply to the court for a 'penal notice' to be attached to the court order. If a person fails to comply with an order which is subject to a penal notice, then it is possible that they could be committed to prison.

Failing to disclose assets

The courts are particularly harsh in dealing with anyone who is found to have failed to make full and frank disclosure of their financial circumstances. Usually there is a significant reduction in what that person might otherwise have received in a property distribution.

If you have not disclosed the details of property owned overseas, the court could take that property into account, make its own assumptions about the value of the property (be it real estate, valuables, investments, bank accounts or any other form of property) and deduct that amount, or whatever it considers appropriate, from your final distribution.

Possible impact on court orders or Separation Deed

The court has the power to overturn orders or a Separation Deed and make new orders if you have not made a full and frank disclosure.

For example, if you fail to disclose an interest in a property and the non-disclosure came to the notice of your former partner after orders had been made, they could apply to have those orders overturned.

WARNING

Disclosure of your financial assets, in EVERY detail, is one of the most important things you have to do.

The moral is: tell the truth and the whole truth about your financial circumstances.

The consequences of non-disclosure may be dire and given the enormous power of the courts to examine your financial affairs, the chances of being caught are high. Don't take the risk. Disclose all of your financial information and get matters resolved and settled properly.

Some specific issues to consider regarding property settlement

The laws around property issues are extensive. When deciding how to deal with your finances after separation, you may want to consider the following:

Legal costs in family matters

The standard rule in family law matters is that each person, or party, pays their own legal costs.

However, in certain exceptional circumstances, the court may order one party to pay the other party's legal costs. Generally, the court takes into account the following:

- ▸ The financial circumstances of each party.
- ▸ The conduct of the parties in the proceedings.
- ▸ Whether either party has failed to comply with previous court orders.
- ▸ Whether any open settlement offer has been made.
- ▸ Any false allegation or statement in the proceedings, and
- ▸ Any other fact relevant to the case.

If the conduct of one person is particularly obstructive, or is such that it warrants a harsher penalty, the court may order them to pay all of the other person's costs that have been 'reasonably and properly incurred'. These are known as indemnity costs.

Disposing of property and the concept of 'add-back'

A court may 'add-back' to the marital pot any amount spent by a party that should have formed part of the property pool. Courts will not always allow add-back arguments and they will not succeed in each and every divorce, particularly if the assets are limited.

You should not sell or dispose of any asset before a property settlement has taken place without agreement from the other party or from the court, even though the asset may be in your name alone. Remember, until the property has been legally distributed between you, "what is mine is ours, what is yours is ours and what is ours is ours"!

If you do dispose of property without prior approval, the value of that property may be 'added back' to your share of the proceeds on distribution. In other words, you will be regarded as having already received the value of that property as part of your final entitlement. Take a situation, for example, where you are entitled to a 50/50 share and the total assets are worth £200,000. If you remove £50,000 from a bank account and fail to account for it, your property distribution will probably be reduced to £50,000 (50 per cent equals £100,000, less the £50,000 you are deemed to have received).

This situation can arise if one party deals with property for their own benefit; that is, removes or disposes of property that would otherwise be part of the assets available for division between both of you. The general rule is that assets that were dealt with recklessly or spent for one person's benefit should be considered as already received in the property settlement by the party who received the benefit (and 'added back'). This may apply whether the assets were dealt with in such a way before or after separation.

A court will not automatically 'add-back' an amount just because it has been spent. Each case will be considered on its own facts and the court will always look at the circumstances of how the money was spent. One party may have savings at separation but no income to pay day-to-day living expenses. It is most unlikely that a court would consider the spending of this money as an improper reduction of the assets to be 'added back' as part of your share. The court is unlikely to 'add-back' where the assets are used to meet reasonable daily needs.

As a general rule, if you lose (or gain) money or assets during the relationship, the losses (or gains) will be shared between you. Under some circumstances, one of you may be held responsible for losses (but it will be rare for one party only to benefit from the wins). You may be held responsible, for example, if one of you acted deliberately to reduce the value of an asset, or acted recklessly or negligently, resulting in a reduction in value.

The same may apply to any assets disposed of between separation and final settlement. If you dispose of an asset for your own benefit, the value of that asset might be 'added back' to the marital pot.

There are many different situations where the court has decided to 'add-back' the value of assets; for example, giving an asset to a friend for no charge or gambling joint money away.

You may use joint money to pay legal costs. Legal fees are considered a reasonable expense and they generally will not be 'added back' into the marital pot. However, each case is decided on its own facts and there may be an adjustment where one party spends significantly more than the other on their lawyers.

Deliberately reducing the value of property

Separation usually places people under stress and they often behave accordingly. Be aware that behaviour that has the effect of reducing the value (or existence) of the assets may have serious consequences. It may attract the 'add-back' principle.

The court will take into account the conduct of a person who deliberately reduces the value of, or wastes, property. Selling the new BMW for £1 is not recommended, nor is slashing tailor made clothes with a razor or throwing your hard-earned cash across the tables at the casino.

Where one person deliberately incurs business losses, the value of those losses may be 'added back' to the marital pot.

Gambling losses can be a little more complicated and, again, each case will depend on its own facts. It can be difficult to maintain an argument that gambling losses should be added back, especially if they generally accepted gambling as a form of entertainment during the relationship, even if it was only done by one of them.

Capital Gains Tax (CGT) can be a trap

Currently, Capital Gains Tax ought not to be payable on the transfer of property if the transfer is done by a property distribution between spouses within the tax year that the parties separate.

However be careful. You may end up with an investment property or some other asset that has increased in value since it was bought. When the property is sold, you will be responsible for payment of all the CGT.

These tax implications should be taken into account when negotiating a property distribution that involves assets where CGT may apply.

If neither party is willing to assume the CGT risk, you should seek to have the relevant asset sold and CGT taken into account as a liability of both parties. The family home will not usually have CGT implications.

Tax liabilities are a potential minefield and need to be carefully thought out. Therefore, you should get sound advice on these issues from an accountant.

Pension entitlements

Either party's pension entitlements can be divided up ('split') and transferred to the other partner as part of a financial distribution. This is known as a Pension Sharing Order.

Pensions are treated as an asset even though they are a future benefit. This is because the pension will generally have been contributed to during the relationship, and this includes not just lump-sum pension entitlements but pensions paid as income in periodic (e.g. monthly) instalments.

You are entitled to receive details of the current value of your former partner's entitlements. This is known as the cash equivalent value.

Pension sharing can only be achieved by way of a court order.

Get legal and financial advice about pension sharing

Unless you have a working knowledge of pensions and this area of the law, you really should get advice before attempting to divide a pension. It is complex and requires professional financial advice. It also demands specialised legal expertise to draft orders, as specific procedures must be followed.

When dealing with pensions, you might be dealing with quite substantial amounts. It may be worth the expense of engaging an actuary or financial adviser and a specialist family lawyer to get it right.

A last word about finalising property distribution by agreement

Consult a lawyer

With financial matters you have the freedom to make an arrangement between yourselves without going to court. Whilst you don't have to use a lawyer, how else will you know whether what you are agreeing to is fair and reasonable? How will you be sure that the final court order does what you want it to do and prevent your other half from coming back for a second bite of the cherry?

Settle sooner, rather than later

You can start negotiating a property settlement from the moment you decide to separate. Consider the following:

▸ The sooner you start, the more likely you are to reach an agreement with your former partner.

▸ Discussions between the two of you are a lot cheaper than an argument conducted by lawyers.

▸ The more you spend on lawyers, the less you will have to divide between yourselves.

▸ It is better to compromise early – rather than see even more of your assets disappear in legal fees and court costs.

Legal fees

It is very important to realise that there are usually no winners in the matrimonial proceedings and paying your own legal expenses is the normal outcome. So you must consider the costs you will incur in running a legal case.

Legal fees are discussed in more detail in chapter 10 'The elephant in the room – legal costs in Family Law matters'.

Use lawyers to draft Financial Agreements and Consent Orders

If you do not use lawyers to reach an agreement, at the very least get lawyers involved to draw up any agreements you're able to reach as a Consent Order and get advice about how to ensure the documents are legal and enforceable.

If you shop around, you should be able to get a fixed fee quote for this work. Although the cost may be several hundred pounds, this is not out of proportion to the work required or the outcome that you will achieve, especially compared with the enormous expense of preparing for and going through a court case.

Litigation might cost you tens (if not hundreds) of thousands of pounds and, even at the end of the case, you might not get anywhere near what you wanted because the court did not see things your way.

An agreement reached between you will:

▸   Slash your legal bills to a fraction of the cost of going to court.

▸   Reduce the time that your life is placed on hold, and

▸   Immediately ease the stress and tensions on you and your family (without such an agreement, you may have to wait many months for a final outcome).

Whatever happens, do not let your lawyer commence court action without telling you about the costs and the likely results. If you can identify the issues early on, you can probably discuss them and negotiate a reasonable settlement, which you can then document as Consent Orders.

On the other hand, if you have millions of pounds worth of assets and you and your ex-partner are in dispute over the value of those assets, and how they should be divided, you may think it is worthwhile to battle it out in court.

In some cases, particularly where the issues are extremely complex or contentious, the courts may have to get involved to sort them out.

TIPS ABOUT PROPERTY ISSUES

Aim to keep as much of the personal property as you can. The cost of replacing personal property will always vastly exceed its 'value' in calculations, which is second-hand auction value. For example, a brand new fridge that cost you £800 might be worth £100 if you auction it.

There are lots of ways of splitting personal property (furniture, paintings, cookware, etc). One approach is using 'coloured spots', where each party has a box of coloured sticky spots and you take turns to put a spot on an item of property until every item has your or their colour on it indicating who gets to keep what in the settlement.

Get financial advice about how realistic proposals are. You may really want to keep the family home, but if you don't have the income to pay off the mortgage, it may not be practical for you to do so. Even if you can pay off the mortgage with your income after the split, how much will be left over for you to live on?

Make sure you get legal advice quickly if there is a danger that your ex-partner might dispose of an asset you might not be able to get back. Although some things can be 'added back' into the marital pot (as discussed earlier in this chapter), specific items might be personally irreplaceable to you.

Don't think you can remove property from a distribution by transferring it out of your name or 'giving' it to another person. The court can slice right through these sorts of manoeuvres.

GETTING IT SETTLED
– IT'S IN YOUR INTERESTS

SUMMARY

▶ Negotiating a settlement agreement with your former partner that both of you can live with is likely to save you a lot of money, time and stress.

▶ Settling will be quicker, easier, cheaper and probably get you closer to what you want than a court decision will.

▶ If possible, it is best to stay out of court and sort things out between you.

▶ If you and your former partner are already in agreement, or close to agreement, lawyers can help you get settlements put in place in a legal way without going to court.

▶ If you think you could reach an agreement but emotions are running high or there are a few things that you can't figure out together, you may wish to consider mediation or hiring a lawyer to help you find new ways to resolve the situation, for example by using collaborative law.

▶ Even if you go to court, you can still decide to come to an agreement with your ex. This can be done even in the middle of a trial – though, obviously, earlier is better (and thousands of pounds cheaper).

Getting matters settled by negotiated agreement is almost always in everybody's best interests. It may be hard, as emotions are raw after a separation, but if it can be achieved, the outcome is likely to be much better than the alternatives.

Let's look in depth at two important questions:

> ▸ **Why** should you seek to settle by negotiated agreement?

> ▸ **How** can you achieve that agreement?

Why try to settle?

A negotiated agreement has many advantages:

> ▸ It gives you finality and certainty. You can then get on with your life knowing what your financial future is likely to be and what arrangements are in place for the kids.

> ▸ It minimises the risks associated with the court processes. No lawyer can promise you what result they will achieve at the end of the process; there are too many unknowns.

> ▸ Your children will not have to live with the ongoing tensions of a court battle (even if it's not about them).

> ▸ Family and close friends will not get dragged into an on going battle.

> ▸ Resolution will be much quicker. Going through the court system can take years (although many matters are resolved more quickly).

> ▸ It will definitely be much less expensive. Lawyers normally charge by the amount of time they spend on your matter, not by the results they achieve. So, the longer your matter goes on, the more it will cost.

> ▸ Starting litigation means you are handing over decisions on important financial and children's issues to somebody else – namely, the Judge. You therefore no longer have any control over the outcome.

> ▸ The legal costs saved by early compromise may more than compensate for the amount that you 'gave away'.

> ▸ In children's matters, a reasonable compromise may well mean that the arrangements work more smoothly for everyone; even though you may have less time with the children than you originally wanted.

How to settle

The steps to a final agreed settlement might proceed as follows:

1. After separation you negotiate a settlement.

2. Successful negotiation leads to:

    a. An Agreement recorded in a Separation Deed, or

    b. A Consent Order.

3. To become binding and enforceable, Consent Orders need to be approved by the court. (However, this can be done on paper and usually does not involve a court attendance).

4. The matter is finalised.

The flowchart below illustrates how the process works:

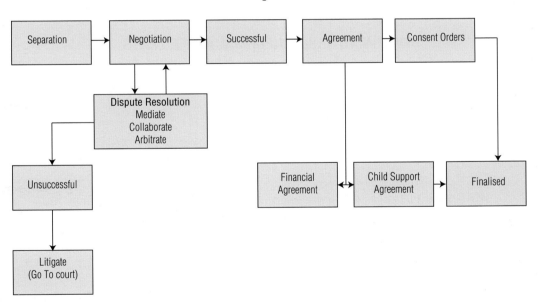

Negotiated settlement

A negotiated settlement means that you determine the terms of agreement, with or without legal or other professional help (such as mediators, or collaborative lawyers). That agreement is then converted into a document that is legally binding.

The agreement is then sent to court as a draft Consent Order and once it is approved by a judge it becomes a final and enforceable contract between you. If both parents agree, Child Support Agreements can be included in the terms of the Consent Order and prevent either party referring the case to the CMS for 12 months following the date of the Consent Order.

You can, of course, simply come to an informal agreement with your ex (whether it's in writing or not) and get on with your business. But such an agreement would not be binding or enforceable (see the box 'A warning about informal agreements' below).

A WARNING ABOUT INFORMAL AGREEMENTS

You can reach an agreement with your ex-partner (in writing or verbally) and leave it at that.

This is known as an 'informal agreement' and is not binding on the parties or legally enforceable.

Whether the agreement will work depends entirely on the continuing good faith of both parties. If one decides they don't like the agreement and decides to take it to court, the informal agreement is nothing more than evidence of your intention at the time it was made.

It is very important to know that either party may seek to have entirely new arrangements made at some later date by applying to the court.

For any agreement to be a legally binding agreement it must be drafted into a Consent Order and approved by a judge

Settlement – how to get it done properly

You can achieve virtually anything by an agreement with your ex-partner, so long as it's legal!

1. **Firstly**, enter into negotiations with your ex-partner. This is often a difficult thing to do, as emotions are high soon after separation. Negotiations usually don't get easier as time progresses and, if you want a negotiated settlement, the sooner you start the better. It is important at this stage to focus on outcomes – getting matters resolved – rather than the blame game of whose fault it was that the relationship did not work. Sometimes, you will only be able to conduct these negotiations through independent and objective third parties.

2. **Secondly**, try to work out the terms of the agreement. You will need to deal with all of the issues that are of concern to you, starting with the ones that are less likely to be in dispute. In this way, you can start building the foundations for agreement with some positive 'can-do' issues, rather than tougher issues that could take longer to resolve.

3. **Thirdly**, get the terms of your understanding put into a legal framework (usually by getting a Consent Order approved by the court) so that the agreement is legally effective and can be implemented in the best possible way.

Need help?

Decide whether you want professional assistance for any or all of these steps. For example, you might ask whether it's worth:

▸   Finding a mediator to assist in your negotiations.

▸   Involving your accountant or financial adviser in understanding the implications of specific terms in the agreement.

▸   Talking to an estate agent about property values and selling or keeping a property.

▸   Seeking assistance from a counsellor or psychologist to help you deal with difficult emotional issues that may arise after separation, and/or

> ▸ Getting lawyers involved in drafting up an agreement or explaining the legal implications of what you propose to include.

Without professional legal assistance you may find it quite difficult to finalise your dispute by writing up an agreement as a Consent Order for lodging in court.

Whether you engage mediators, accountants, lawyers or any other professionals at any stage is really a cost-benefit analysis that only you can undertake.

As far as legal involvement is concerned, you might want to think about the following questions:

> ▸ How much will the lawyers cost? (This is a question you should always ask your lawyer at the outset.)

> ▸ Is this cost fixed and guaranteed or is it an estimate? If so, what is the top end of the range that you might be asked to pay and are there any caps or limits on what you might be charged?

> ▸ Are there any additional fees (such as court costs or barristers' fees) to be included and how much are they likely to be?

> ▸ How much is it worth to have the peace of mind of knowing everything has been finally and legally resolved?

> ▸ Is it worth the legal expense if the asset pool is relatively modest or you are dealing with quite a simple issue?

> ▸ Do the arrangements proposed for the children require consideration and careful drafting by a lawyer or are they so straightforward that the expense would not be justified?

> ▸ Are there any complicated issues regarding property that a lawyer should look through?

> ▸ Are you getting a property deal that is fair and reasonable in the eyes of the law and that has everything that should be included?

> ▸ Are pensions involved, and if so, should you be seeking a transfer of part of your ex-partner's pension entitlements or should you be giving them part of yours? What should the mix of pension and non-pension assets be?

At the end of the day, whether or not you involve a lawyer is your decision.

Whatever else you do, don't forget our earlier advice: unless your agreement is prepared in accordance with specific requirements, you do not have a binding and enforceable contract. Ask yourself the question: **"Is it worth running that risk?"**

What are Consent Orders?

Consent Orders can be made at any time after Decree Nisi by the court. They are usually made in one of two circumstances:

▸ As a result of filing an Application for Consent Orders without disputed proceedings, or

▸ At any stage during disputed proceedings commenced by one of the parties.

Application for Consent Orders

If you and your ex-partner are able to reach an agreement about property distribution (with or without legal assistance), you can file (lodge) that agreement at court for the judge to approve.

The court will then review the orders that you are seeking. In relation to financial and property matters, if satisfied that the terms of the agreement are 'fair and reasonable' and otherwise appropriate, the court will approve the draft order and seal it.

Consent Orders during court proceedings

After you have commenced proceedings in court, it is still possible to settle any (or all) of the disputed issues by asking the court to make a Consent Order in whatever terms you agree.

If you are seeking to finalise all of the disputed issues, the court will again want to satisfy itself that the terms are fair and reasonable before issuing a Final Order and concluding the court process.

Using a lawyer

Unless you are seeking very simple and straightforward orders – it is certainly quicker, safer and probably a lot less expensive in the long term to use a good lawyer to draw up the documents and obtain the Consent Orders that you need.

Other do-it-yourself kits

Several DIY kits (which are not produced by the Family Court) claim to take you through the process of creating and filing Consent Orders to divide your property or make arrangements for your children. Be careful as they might land you in hot water.

Setting out and documenting proper arrangements for your children and financial distribution can be a minefield for people without professional training and legal knowledge. Many lawyers with years of experience in general practice but no family law specialisation have difficulty giving advice on these matters or finding their way through the documentation required.

Doing your own divorce

Information regarding divorce procedure is also available on the court website. The guidance details the divorce process and which forms to use when. Most divorce forms can now be downloaded from the court website, or hard copies can be obtained from the court office.

Doing your own divorce can be straightforward, but be careful to comply with all of the instructions, fill out the forms exactly as required and follow the procedures carefully. If you don't, it will cost you money to put right.

When in doubt, get some legal advice. It is likely to be helpful, save you a lot of time and be well worth the money you pay for it.

IF IT POSITIVELY, DEFINITELY HAS TO GO TO COURT

SUMMARY

▸   Court proceedings usually take a long time, are expensive and can be emotionally exhausting. They can go on for months, sometimes years.

▸   There are several stages to the court process. You don't just turn up once and your case is over. There can be several hearings to settle the matter on the way before you get to the final Trial.

▸   Did we say expensive? Going to court can be VERY EXPENSIVE. Depending on how far into the process it goes, it is likely to cost several thousands of pounds, and, in some cases, the legal fees can run into hundreds of thousands of pounds.

▸   Your lawyer should give you an estimate of what your particular case will cost, they may also be able to offer a fixed fee.

▸   Alternatively, you can run your own case in court and represent yourself. This may be difficult and time consuming and, if you don't get it right, there can be some pretty serious consequences.

Going to court

Litigation means going to court. This chapter explains the court process and provides some hints on how to deal with it.

The courts that deal with such issues have websites setting out their procedures, information, forms to download and 'how to' guides. Have a look at the sites because this book only provides a simplified description of the court system.

Additionally, an organisation called "Resolution", which represents the majority of specialist family law solicitors nationwide, has a number of guides and protocols that can go a long way to helping couples resolve their disputes without actively involving the court system.

Indeed, most separations never reach the courts. Many are resolved by the parties without ever seeing a lawyer, especially where there are few assets to 'divvy up' and the couple can resolve issues about the kids. However, sometimes you will end up in the court no matter how hard you try to avoid it.

Litigation is not pleasant and it can be a long and expensive process. It can also leave deep and lasting scars on you and on your relationships with others.

The litigation process is adversarial, which means that each disputing party puts their opposing cases before the court. You put your best case forward and the other party does the same. It is inevitable that each side also paints the worst possible picture of the other's case.

Family law gives Judges and Magistrates wide discretionary powers. Therefore, a "win-lose" result is uncommon. Although the aim for the court is to reach a fair overall settlement, this can often feel like a "lose-lose" outcome, with neither of you ending up with everything you want. Both can end up worse off than if you had negotiated a settlement at the outset, especially after costs are taken into account.

We generally refer to the people involved in court proceedings as 'the parties'. This is the legal description of those on opposing sides. There are rare occasions when more than just ex-partners may be parties to the dispute. 'Third parties' might become involved where their interests are mixed up with the outcome of your issues; for example, creditors, relations, a company or a trust.

The court process simplified

It is important to realise that there are various processes depending on the type of litigation contemplated. The court process for dealing with financial disputes arising on divorce (or civil partnership dissolution) is very different to that which unmarried couples would go through. Just to make things even more difficult, litigation over children involves a further different court process. For the sake of simplicity, therefore, this chapter will deal solely with the first of these litigation processes, namely financial issues arising on divorce or dissolution.

The diagram 'Simplified court process' below illustrates the basic court process, from the start of proceedings until final resolution by a Judge.

SIMPLIFIED COURT PROCESS

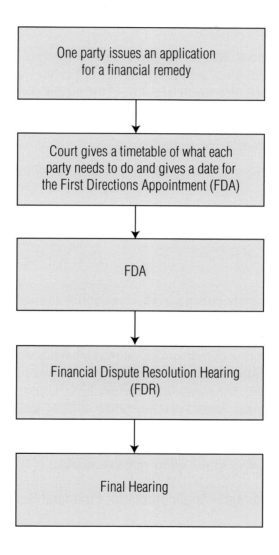

You cannot start financial proceedings without divorce proceedings. As divorces are dealt with by the County Courts, most financial cases are dealt with there too. Usually, this will be the court that is nearest geographically to where you live, although sometimes it may be further away, perhaps closer to where your ex or one of the solicitors is based. You can issue in any County Court in England and Wales.

Jurisdiction

Issues relating to financial matters on divorce or dissolution will automatically fall under the court's jurisdiction, assuming the court has the power to deal with the divorce in the first place. Practically speaking, this means that:

> The court has been given the power under the Matrimonial Causes Act 1973 to determine these matters.

> You are a person who is allowed to start the court proceedings in question.

This is why you must have issued divorce proceedings either prior to, or at the same time as, issuing financial proceedings.

The court process

It is important to remember that for all cases going through the court system at any level (whether about children or money), the court has a duty to consider alternative methods for the parties to resolve their dispute. The reason is twofold: firstly it will speed the process up and provide the parties with an outcome sooner rather than later; secondly, it will reduce cost. The buzzword today is "mediation". Not all cases are suitable for mediation; for example, where there is violence, but other than in exceptional cases everyone must at least attempt to go through a Mediation Information and Assessment Meeting (MIAM) prior to issuing formal court proceedings. Even once proceedings have started, the duty to consider mediation as an alternative to the court remains in place.

Commencing proceedings – Applications for Financial Remedy

Court proceedings start with one party making an Application for Financial Remedy to the court.

The form, known as a "Form A" simply indicates your intention to deal with the various types of remedy that are available to both parties on divorce or dissolution.

If you are making an application for interim maintenance as well, you will also need to submit a short statement setting out what you seek and why you think you should receive it. You can find the Form A on the court website.

The application and any accompanying documents are then 'filed' in the court, which means that at least three copies of all the documents have to be taken to the court. The court officers will then 'stamp' the documents to show this has been done. They will keep one copy for the court records, give you back one copy for yourself and send out the third copy to the other party. This is what is known as "service". This does not have to be done in person; you can simply put the documents in the post.

The court will also provide a further document that sets out a timetable leading up to the First Directions Appointment (FDA) and, if necessary, a separate date to deal with interim maintenance. The court currently has a duty to fix the date for the FDA between 12 and 16 weeks from the date of the Application. The court will also set a timetable for you both to file and exchange formal disclosure of your financial assets, using Form E, which is a standard court document. That date will be 5 weeks before the FDA. Then, 2 weeks before the FDA, you must file and exchange various documents that will assist the court in understanding and narrowing the issues and what further information may be required, to help resolve your case.

Responses

If you are on the receiving end of an Application for Financial Remedy, you need to comply with the court's timetable or you run the risk of the court making orders sought by the other party, including costs orders should you fail to comply with the directions.

Court fees

Don't forget the courts also charge fees at certain stages of the family law process. Find out what they are from the court website or ask your lawyer to provide the relevant information.

COURT FEES

To get up-to-date information on fees, check the court website
www.justice.gov.uk/courts/fees

Prior to the First Directions Appointment (FDA)

Whether you are the Applicant or the Respondent, you should both stick to the dates set in the court timetable in the lead up to the FDA. This will mean that your case has the best chance of reaching a successful early settlement. The steps you will need to take are as follows:

▸ Complete your financial disclosure. This is done using a document called a Form E Financial Statement. This document will be sent to you by the court as part of the application pack together with notes on how to complete it and what documents you will need in support.

▸ Exchange Forms E once you know that both are filed at court.

▸ Prepare the documents required by the court prior to the FDA.

▸ These are:

  ▸ Chronology – setting out important and relevant dates that the court needs to know.

  ▸ Statement of Issues – so the court will have an understanding as to what the key factors are.

  ▸ Questionnaire – asking for further information or clarification of your ex-partner's financial disclosure.

  ▸ Form G – telling the court whether the parties are ready to negotiate yet.

  ▸ Form H – setting out what your legal fees are up to and including the hearing.

The FDA

The first time you are likely to be required to attend court is for the FDA. The date, time and the address for the FDA will be notified on the first page of the court's timetable sent to both parties after the application has been issued. The hearing is most likely to take place before a District Judge in Chambers – a room that may look more like a large office than a courtroom.

If there are interim issues to be heard, you should be prepared to argue the matter before the District Judge or give your lawyer all the information required to enable them to argue for you.

In some circumstances, your lawyer may engage a barrister to appear in court for you. Barristers are lawyers who specialise in court work and are often engaged when the issues to be argued in court are complex. Barristers usually charge a fixed fee for attending hearings. Many of them will ask that your lawyer also attend the hearing (so you end up paying for both to be there).

ATTENDANCE AT COURT HEARINGS AND CONFERENCES

Always check with the court about the requirement to attend the different hearings that may be scheduled. Ask your lawyer (if you have one). If in doubt, attend.

You are entitled to attend every hearing that involves your case and you are required to attend most of them.

If you are representing yourself, you must attend every hearing that is listed.

If both sides have prepared properly, it should be fairly clear to all parties and the Judge where the differences lie. You will have the opportunity to discuss the case with your opponent before the hearing if you wish. This may help you agree on what needs to be done.

The District Judge's role is to work out what (if any) further information the court will need before it can help the parties to negotiate. The focus is very much on trying to reach agreement.

At the end of the FDA, whether interim issues are involved or not, the court will make orders and/or directions about your matter. Take careful note of what has been decided. If you are in any doubt about what is required, or what has been ordered, ask the District Judge to clarify or explain matters to you. Common orders made at FDA hearings are as follows:

▸ Appointing a surveyor to value property (such as the family home) if its value cannot be agreed.

▸ If there are significant pensions, then an actuary or other pension expert may be appointed to provide a report advising upon pension sharing.

▸ If there are business interests, then an accountant may be appointed to provide a report on issues of valuation, liquidity and future income available from businesses.

▸ The court will usually order you and your partner to reply to the other's questionnaire. That is often required to be done within 28 days of the hearing.

▸ On some occasions the court may direct that statements are produced dealing with specific issues which may be in dispute.

▸ The court will fix a date for the next court hearing known as the Financial Dispute Resolution hearing.

Although the court orders will be printed out and sent to you (or your lawyer) after the hearing, it is always sensible to find out at the hearing what is proposed in case you have problems with complying. Otherwise, you may have to ask for another court date to try to undo what was done the first time. This is a waste of everyone's time and, often, your money.

The court orders will almost always specify when the matter will come before the court again.

When in court:

▸ Always treat the court officials with respect. They are just doing their job; which is often a difficult one.

▸ Try not to raise your voice or be argumentative. Never be abusive or insulting towards the other parties or their lawyers, no matter what they might say or do.

> ▶ Every time you appear in court, you are on show and you are creating an impression. Put your best foot forward: present your arguments in a rational and clear way and be calm and controlled at all times.

> ▶ If you do not feel capable of presenting your arguments in a courtroom, engage a lawyer to do it for you; that is their job and they should do it competently and in your best interests.

> ▶ The other advantage of having a lawyer represent you in court is that they will know the processes that will enable your case to be processed as quickly and effectively as possible.

Financial Dispute Resolution Hearing

Financial Dispute Resolution (FDR) hearings are the second stage of the Financial Remedy process. The FDR is a hearing in front of a District Judge. The parties and legal advisors attend with a view to trying again to get matters resolved by way of agreement.

Theoretically, all parties are required to have clearly defined the issues in dispute and, in property matters, exchanged all relevant financial documents before the FDR takes place. Regrettably, this is not always the case and much time and money is wasted where cases are inadequately prepared and the proper processes have not been followed. However, assuming the directions given at the FDA have been complied with, there is no reason why the FDR should not be a very effective tool in narrowing issues with a view to reaching settlement.

You must come prepared to state your case clearly and explain why you want the orders you are asking the court to make. Know your case (and the other party's case), make sure you have read the documents carefully and have specific proposals to get matters resolved or proposals that will move the case forward (such as further disclosure of financial documents). The hearing may seem quite formal but is much less so than any Final Hearing would be.

What is said at an FDR is described as being 'without prejudice'. It can be a bit confusing, but 'without prejudice' is a legal description for comments and statements that may not be repeated in court (especially at the Final Hearing) and used against you. For example, if at the FDR you offered to settle everything on a 50/50 basis just to get it resolved out of court, the other party cannot then repeat that to the Judge at the Final Hearing where you might be seeking a 60/40 distribution in your favour.

It is very important to know that the FDR is "without prejudice". The District Judge who hears the FDR is barred from hearing the Final Hearing and any documents produced for the court specifically for the FDR must be removed from the court file at the end of the FDR.

It is normal for everyone to arrive at court at least an hour before the time the hearing is due to start. This can give time for negotiations to start. If things are looking promising, the District Judge will often step back and allow the negotiations to continue. However, the Judge will not let things run on all day and, if no settlement is reached, will ultimately start the FDR.

Typically, the District Judge will start off the FDR by recommending to each party that they engage in the process, with a warning that if they cannot settle, there will be further delays, costs will increase dramatically and they may be forced to accept a solution imposed on them that neither of them wants.
Both parties then have the chance to put their case and explain why the court should favour their point of view.

After both parties have explained their position, the District Judge is required to offer a "view". Whilst that view is not binding, it may well have the effect of concentrating the minds of both parties.

Sometimes, District Judges will be very direct and tell you that they do not believe the court will make the orders you are seeking. Some will simply advise each of the parties to think carefully about the costs of what they are doing, suggest that no one will get exactly what they want and point out that there are no guarantees in the court process.

After consideration of the issues, the District Judge may "stand down" your case and request that the parties leave the room to see whether they can resolve the matter and return with a draft order of what has been agreed.

If you have managed to make progress, many District Judges will continue the FDR to try to bring your positions closer together in the hope of achieving a resolution. Sometimes this happens, sometimes it doesn't. If matters can be resolved at this stage (whether entirely or in part) an order can be drafted and approved by the District Judge on the basis of what you have agreed.

If a final agreement cannot be reached, the District Judge will make further orders regarding what needs to be done to prepare for a Final Hearing (also referred to as a trial).

The court will set a trial date and allocate the time required to hear all the evidence. This may be a day or it may be significantly longer, depending on the issues that are to be argued, the number of witnesses, the evidence that is to be presented, and similar issues.

The aim is to get all the matters heard at one time, to allow the Judge to then make a fully informed decision on all issues.

Final Hearing

The Final Hearing is your opportunity to present the evidence in support of the orders you want the Judge to make and to tell the Judge why those orders should be made.

Once all of the evidence has been given by all of the parties, the Judge will be able to make a decision that deals with all of the issues in dispute.

This is the last opportunity you will get, so make sure you get it right and present the best case you can.

PRESENTING YOUR CASE AT TRIAL

Think carefully about going to trial without getting legal advice.

At the Final Hearing, you will have to make submissions to the court based on the law and its application to parts of, or to all of, the case you are putting forward.

Therefore, if you are not represented by a lawyer at this stage, you could be at a significant disadvantage.

The court will give you every opportunity to put forward your case. However, the Judge will not make your case for you or assist you to present the proper legal basis for your case.

Preparing the case for Final Hearing

The three rules of buying real estate are 'location, location and location'. The rule of three also applies to getting ready for a trial, where it becomes 'preparation, preparation and preparation'.

Statements

Your primary evidence at the Final Hearing is given by your Form E Financial Statement that you prepared right at the outset of the proceedings. It is therefore very important to ensure that the document is accurate and truthful. Sometimes the court directs that the parties prepare written narrative statements. The content of that statement depends upon what the issues are between you. The statement will set out the facts of your case. There is no longer a requirement for statements to be sworn but they do contain a "Statement of Truth". They are the written equivalent of the evidence that you give verbally when you appear in court: 'the truth, the whole truth and nothing but the truth'.

A separate statement is usually required from each of the parties and from every witness who will be called in support of the respective cases.

Preparation of the Form E Financial Statement and any narrative statement is one of the most important aspects of your whole case. It is the primary evidence you are putting before the court to enable the Judge to make a decision in your favour. Preparing good evidence requires skill and care and can be very time consuming. All of the relevant issues have to be covered and all of the facts have to be stated accurately. Irrelevant information should be avoided. Argument should be avoided; you are not making your argument in your statement but simply stating the facts that are relevant to the case you are putting to the Judge. Arguments made in a statement will be ignored and will probably only irritate the Judge who has to read them.

The length of your trial statement is not the key. The really important issue is presenting in a coherent and logical way those facts that are relevant to the outcome you seek.

You must consider the position you intend to put forward at the Final Hearing and what evidence supports that case or undermines the case of the other party. So, you have to work backwards; start with the result you want and then work back to what you have to prove in order to support that result.

For example, if you want the Judge to give you a greater share of the assets than the other person, work out what legal principles support that conclusion (such as a greater contribution at the start of the relationship) and then set out the facts upon which you rely (such as evidence of assets you had before the relationship began).

There is a real skill in preparing good statements; if you follow a logical and methodical process, you will be more likely to convince the Judge than by just blurting it all out.

This is where lawyers really come into their own, helping you gather and present evidence. They usually know what is relevant and supports your case, and the best way to present the arguments.

Preparing for the hearing

Preparing for court hearings requires planning for what lies ahead. Here are some things you could do to make sure that you are properly prepared:

> ▸ Make sure you understand the evidence you will give and that you have read and re-read all of the evidence that you have provided.

> ▸ Make sure you meet your solicitor and/or barrister before the hearing to talk over the matter.

> ▸ Listen carefully to your lawyer's advice about the proper way to give evidence and to answer questions in court. Generally, the formula is to answer questions directly and simply, without going into lengthy explanations.

Finally, the day has arrived

Your lawyer will be wearing a suit, as will the Judge. How you dress should show respect for the court. Suits, even jackets, are not essential but often preferable. On the other hand, dirty clothes, work clothes or ripped jeans are unlikely to endear you to the Judge – even if you intend to show how hard-working or impoverished you are. Dress neatly and comfortably in smart casual clothing.

Attend the court well ahead of the hearing time so that you can discuss any last-minute issues with your lawyers and get the feel of the courtroom where your case is being heard. Check and re-check the hearing time and also the location of the court.

Do not bring children to court, unless ordered to do so as most courts do not have facilities for them. It is widely considered that courts are not good places for children. After all, they may well see their parents in conflict with each other. The best advice is to leave them at home with a carer.

The hearing itself

At the Final Hearing, each party presents their case to the court in a controlled way. The Judge presiding over the hearing has a broad discretion as to how the proceedings will be conducted, subject to the requirements of law and the rules of evidence that apply to that court.

Throughout much of the hearing, you will hear the parties referred to as 'the Applicant' and 'the Respondent'. If you commenced the legal proceedings, you are the Applicant. Otherwise, you are the Respondent. There may be more than one Respondent if third parties have been included in the proceedings (by their own choice or because one of the parties has included them). In almost all cases, the Applicant presents their case first and, when this process is complete, the Respondent presents their case.

Each party's primary evidence is presented by the statements and other documents that have already been filed in the court and copied to all parties. So, in theory at least, you cannot surprise the other party with a last-minute disclosure of something unknown.

A trial is usually opened by the Applicant's barrister presenting an outline of the case (the Opening). Then the Applicant gives their evidence; firstly by their own barrister asking questions (this is known as "Evidence in Chief") and then by the other party (or, more usually, the other party's barrister). This is "cross examination" and gives the other side the opportunity to test the evidence that the Applicant has presented. Then each of the Applicant's witnesses (who have provided statements and whose evidence the other side wants to question) will be called and will give their evidence. If a witness fails to appear when called, the Judge may disregard the contents of their statement.

Questioning is usually conducted by the barrister representing the other side and is called cross-examination. Barristers are usually very skilled and can undermine a person's credibility if their evidence is not accurate and truthful.

No matter how you feel about matters that are discussed during the hearing, do your best not to react to what is said by a witness or the lawyer (or, especially, the Judge). You may think what is being said is incorrect or deliberately misleading but it is up to your legal team, not you, to deal with what arises. Even though it may be hard not to react, you should simply listen. If you don't understand what has happened, ask your lawyer to explain.

If something is said that is untruthful, and this point has not previously been discussed with your legal team (and is of significance and importance), make a note and let your lawyer know. If you are running your own case, raise the matter in cross-examination of the relevant witness or mention the fact in your address to the Judge.

When you are called to give evidence

You don't have to state again to the court all of what's said in your statement, as the Judge will have read that document (and all the other statements submitted) and will already know what you claim to be the truth.

You will be asked to swear or affirm that your evidence will be truthful. In most cases, your lawyer will then 'tidy up' any loose ends in your statement. They may clarify some elements that are not clear, adjust a statement that might not be entirely accurate or update information that has come to hand after the statement was made. This is what is known as giving "Evidence in Chief".

Then the other party's lawyer will question (cross-examine) you about what is in your statement and any other part of the case that is being considered by the court. This questioning can be very wide ranging and is likely to be quite detailed. Sometimes, the questioning can go on for many hours (even days). Bearing the following points in mind might help:

▸ If you need a break, ask the Judge for one.

▸ Try to stay composed and alert to what is being asked.

▸ Do not lose your cool. It does not help your case to get into an argument with the barrister (who, after all, is just doing their job).

▸ If you can, relax. Even when the barrister is trying to pick holes in your evidence. If you have told the truth in your statement, you have nothing to be concerned about.

▶ Focus on the questions and answer them in a straightforward and direct way.

▶ Do not go into detail unless you are specifically asked to do so.

▶ If a "yes" or "no" is required, just give that answer and no more.

▶ Do not try to 'out-think' the barrister and second-guess what they are trying to find out.

▶ Reply to the questions as you understand them. If you do not fully understand a question, ask the barrister to explain or to ask it again.

▶ Do not use it as an opportunity to argue your case. That is your lawyer's job.

During your cross examination, there may be occasions when your lawyer stands up and interrupts the questioning. This will happen if your lawyer believes the questioning is not appropriate for some reason. When this happens, do not get involved, unless asked to by the Judge. Simply wait until the Judge sorts things out.

The Judge may ask you questions from time to time as well. Listen carefully and, as with all questions put to you, answer directly and honestly.

When the other party's lawyer has finished questioning you, your own lawyer may ask you a few further questions (called 're-examination') to clarify aspects of your evidence.

When that is finished, your evidence to the court is over. You will not have to return to give further evidence (except in exceptional circumstances).

Telling the truth in court

Telling lies in court proceedings, whether it is what you put in your statement or what you say when giving evidence in court, is called 'perjury'. Perjury is a criminal offence and can result in imprisonment.

While jail terms are not usual, telling untruths in the family court has other consequences. The most obvious is that your credibility is damaged and, as a result, all of your evidence comes into question. This may result in your case falling apart, simply because your evidence is not believed and the other person's version of the facts is preferred.

You should stick to the facts when giving evidence. Don't embellish the story by adding bits that aren't true.

Tell the whole truth. Don't try to hide or avoid parts of the evidence that might not do you great credit. No one is perfect and we have all made many mistakes in life. Judges understand this. They are not there to judge your character or moral behaviour. The weak spots in your case will have to be dealt with, just as much as the highlights.

After all the Applicant's witnesses have been called, the same happens with the Respondent and their witnesses, (if any) who will be cross-examined by the Applicant's lawyer.

When the Respondent's witnesses have each had their stint in the witness box, each party closes its case. They do this by presenting submissions to the Judge about the evidence, the law and the conclusions they want the Judge to make as a result of what has been revealed at the Final Hearing.

You may be at a significant disadvantage presenting your final submission if you do not have a firm grasp of the law and the relevant rules of evidence. That is why parties are usually represented by lawyers (usually a solicitor and a barrister) in matters that go to a Final Hearing.

When the Final Hearing is over

After the Final Hearing has concluded, you wait for the Judge to make a decision.

Sometimes the Judge will make a Final Order as soon as the parties have concluded final presentations.

Sometimes the Judge will adjourn the matter for a decision to be delivered at some stage in the future.

Final Orders

The end of the court process is the issuing of orders by the Judge. This is when you are told what the Judge has decided and what they determine is to happen with financial distribution. That's it. No arguments, unless you want to appeal (and that is another costly and lengthy process).

How long will it all take?

The court process can take a long time from start to finish. If your matter is not unduly complex and goes through all the steps to Final Hearing, it is likely to take at least nine months in the County Court (and much longer in the High Court). But most matters will settle earlier and not go all the way through the process to a trial. However, if your matter is complex, it may take much longer.

At each court hearing, you will be advised when the next court hearing is likely to be, but don't be surprised if there are adjournments or delays along the way. Your lawyer should be able to give you updates and time estimates as the matter progresses, but there is no guarantee that the court will be able to dispose of all the matters that are listed and when they are scheduled.

Getting off the court treadmill

Don't despair. You can settle your matter at any time, even if the Final Hearing has started.

Being involved in litigation does not put you on a treadmill that you can never get off. Indeed, the court process is designed to promote settlement rather than dispute. It should help to concentrate everyone's minds, providing a framework and timetable within which negotiations can take place. You can settle with your ex-partner at any time during the litigation process. As we said at the start of this chapter, most cases do not go to court at all. Of those that do, the vast majority of cases settle at or shortly after the FDR stage and only a very small percentage end up needing a contested Final Hearing and a decision by the Judge.

So, if you end up in court, be alert to the possibility of getting your matter resolved as soon as possible through a sensible and pragmatic compromise. The longer you go on, the more it will cost and the more impact on involved parties; not to mention the collateral damage to children, extended family and friends.

Keep trying to get your differences settled. Once you have reached an agreement you can apply to the court to make a Consent Order at any stage in the proceedings.

Complying with court orders

Once the court makes an order it is legally binding and you must follow it.

There are penalties and sanctions for failing to comply with court orders. If you do not follow orders, you also leave yourself open to potential costs orders against you, which may run to thousands of pounds.

The court does not look kindly on those who take the law into their own hands, so you would be well advised to read court orders carefully. If you do not understand them or are unsure about their full meaning, ask the Judge to explain or seek legal advice about your responsibilities.

CONTRACTING OUT OF THE FAMILY LAW SYSTEM

SUMMARY

▶ Pre-Nups can be made before the marriage; Post-Marriage contracts during the marriage and Separation Deeds after the marriage or relationship has broken down.

▶ The documents can set out how it is agreed the property will be divided upon relationship breakdown, or if breakdown has occurred, any agreement subsequently reached.

▶ However, being in possession of any of the above does not prevent either of the parties to the agreement making an application for the court to consider the distribution of the property upon eventual divorce or dissolution. Nor does it prevent the courts from intervening in a property distribution, should a court application be made.

▶ The courts can however, have reference to the agreements and their terms. If the court considers that any of these agreements have been prepared fairly and reasonably, with both parties having received independent legal advice and there having been full financial disclosure between the parties, then the court will give them their due consideration.

▶ Often it can be difficult for the court to apply the terms of the agreement fully if there has been a substantial change of circumstances since the agreement was drawn up – for example, the birth of a child.

Pre-Nups and Post-Nups contracts – what they are and what they do

A pre-nuptial agreement ('pre-nup') is entered into before marriage and allows a couple to plan financially should their marriage breakdown. Pre-civil partnership agreements are similar and are available to couples about to enter into a civil partnership.

A post-marriage agreement ('post-nup') is entered into after marriage, while a couple are still together and allows a couple to plan financially should their marriage subsequently breakdown. Civil partners can enter into a post-partnership agreement.

No one wants to believe that their marriage or civil partnership will end in divorce and such agreements are often seen as unromantic and dooming a marriage to failure. In reality however marriages and civil partnerships do break down and having a pre or post-nuptial agreement or pre or post-partnership agreement in place can avoid the time, expense and animosity experienced in many divorce cases.

Current status of the law re: pre-nups and post-nups contracts

Although enforceable in many countries outside the UK, as the law currently stands in England and Wales these agreements are not legally binding and cannot be used to limit or oust the jurisdiction of the divorce court. However, following a Supreme Court decision in 2010, a principle has been established that the court should give effect to a nuptial agreement that is freely entered into by each party with a full appreciation of its implications unless in the circumstances, it would not be fair to hold the parties to their agreement. This case also confirms that no distinction should be made between the legal treatment of pre-nuptial and post-marriage agreements.

What circumstances may render an agreement unfair?

What the court deems fair will depend on the facts of a particular case.

The Supreme Court has given the following general guidance on what is meant by fairness:

- An agreement cannot be allowed to effect the reasonable requirements of any children of the family.

- An agreement should meet the needs of both parties.

- ▶ Where the agreement only addresses the circumstances as at the time of the agreement the court should be slow to interfere with the agreement. Where however an agreement attempts to address all of the future unknowns in married life, it is more likely that what has actually happened will be different, and then the agreement may be seen as unfair.

- ▶ Where a couple enter into the agreement assuming they will each run their own independent professional lives and keep their finances separate but then find this impossible when they have children.

- ▶ Where an older couple enter into an agreement to keep their finances separate but then one becomes the carer or is rendered homeless if grown up children take priority.

- ▶ Where a couple enter into an agreement thinking one will always be the breadwinner and the other the homemaker but then the homemaker's career takes off and the roles are reversed.

What circumstances will influence the weight to be given to an agreement?

The circumstances surrounding the making of an agreement will affect the weight to be given to it upon a divorce. The court has given the following guidance on what circumstances should be taken into account:

- ▶ Whether there is evidence of duress, fraud or misrepresentation.

- ▶ Whether there has been undue pressure or exploitation of a dominant position.

- ▶ Whether the parties to the agreement have taken legal advice.

- ▶ Whether the parties to the agreement have exchanged full disclosure of their assets and income before signing the agreement.

- ▶ Whether each party should intend for the agreement to be binding. Such intention will be assumed.

- ▶ The parties' ages, maturity, previous experience of relationships and marriage will be relevant, as will the question of whether the marriage would have gone ahead without the agreement.

- ▶ Whether the agreement was entered into at least 21 days prior to marriage.

What other safeguards can be put in place?

A change in circumstances or the time that has elapsed since the making of an agreement may render an agreement unfair or reduce the weight to be attached to it. It is therefore a good idea to regularly review and update the agreement.

If the court decides that an agreement is not fair (for example, if it considers that needs have not been met or a party has not been adequately compensated) then the agreement is not scrapped but instead it is amended to bring it within the boundaries of what the court considers fair.

Review of the law

In their consultation paper, Marital Property Agreements, published in 2011, the Law Commission published their recommendations on changes to the law in this area. The subject of their consultation was whether the law should go further by permitting some agreements outside the jurisdiction of the court. This is a step that cannot be taken by the courts; new legislation would be required.

Separation Deeds – what they are and what they do

Separation deeds set out how a couple have agreed the distribution of their financial assets following their separation. They are usually put in place when the couple have separated and have agreed their financial affairs, but do not intend to divorce immediately. The deed should set out any agreement reached regarding eventual divorce and that the Separation Deed will be converted into a Consent Order, upon the divorce.

For all practical purposes, these agreements are the same for married couples and unmarried couples, but a deed prepared following the separation of a cohabiting couple, will clearly not refer to divorce.

Couples (whether in a married or in a cohabiting relationship) may enter into a Separation Deed to deal with financial arrangements following a separation. You can also make arrangements for ongoing financial maintenance for one or both of you in a Separation Deed.

It is important to know that Separation Deeds don't prevent the courts from interfering in the arrangements you have made for property division and financial maintenance upon divorce, should one of the couple make a court application. The deed can't prevent a subsequent court application. But it isn't easy to get a Separation Deed set aside.

The requirements for a Separation Deed include:

▸ Disclosure of the assets and liabilities that are to be covered by the Separation Deed and all relevant financial information.

▸ Before signing, both parties should have obtained independent legal advice about:

  ▸ The effect of the agreement on their rights, and

  ▸ The advantages and disadvantages of the agreement.

  ▸ Both parties must have freely entered into the agreement.

  ▸ Both parties must have signed the agreement.

Why you might want a Pre-Nup, Post-Marriage contract or a Separation Deed

There are many circumstances where one of the above might be desirable. Some of the more obvious ones include:

▸ To provide certainty regarding the outcome if separation occurs.

▸ To avoid arguments down the track.

▸ To preserve the ownership of existing property, but share all jointly acquired assets.

▸ To preserve an existing or anticipated inheritance.

▸ Where one party has much greater wealth than the other.

▸ In second relationships or marriages where the interests of children from former relationships are to be protected.

▸ For asset protection or preservation when there is an early distribution from a potential estate (sometimes called 'inter-generational wealth transfer'), and

> ▸ Trading off a future property distribution against a spousal maintenance arrangement. (For example, one person gets certain property while the other gets the financial security of on going financial support).

Inter-generational asset transfers

Sometimes parents want to transfer some of their assets to their children as a form of 'early inheritance'. If a transfer is made to someone in a relationship, their partner may become entitled to a share of these assets in the event of a separation down the track. Understandably, parents may be reluctant to do the transfer in these circumstances as their intention is to benefit their own child, not necessarily their partner.

The parents can gain some protection if the assets they intend to transfer are included in a Pre-Nup or a Post-Marriage contract.

Why you might not want to enter into a Pre-Nup, Post-Marriage contract or a Separation Deed

One of the potential difficulties with any of the above is that they require a prediction about your financial position at some unknown time in the future if you separate. This is clearly an almost impossible task. Any number of events could intervene to influence the actual position; for example, serious injury to you or your partner, loss of income, unexpected windfalls or changes in family circumstances.

If you separate without an agreement in place, your property distribution will be entirely determined by family law. You will be free to negotiate a settlement with the knowledge of your exact financial position and particular set of circumstances at the date you decide to call it a day. If you can't agree, you can ask the court to intervene.

Specialist legal advice is essential if you want to ensure that any agreement you enter into does what it is you want it to do.

If you are the financially weaker party, it is usually the case that you will receive a greater distribution of property under family law than you would if, in particular, a Pre-Nup or a Post-Marriage contract were in place.

COHABITATION

This chapter could easily be a book in its own right, but what we attempt to do here is give an overview of the type of things to look out for.

Let's start by dispelling an urban myth: there is no such thing as a "common law spouse". You can live with someone for 50 years, but unless you are married you are not entitled to anything purely on the basis that you live together.

At the time of writing, as an unmarried person in a relationship with someone, you are not currently entitled to:

▶ **Spousal maintenance** – unlike married couples cohabitants have no claims against each other's income, so if you jointly own a property with your partner and they fail to pay the mortgage, you cannot apply to court to have them pay their share of the mortgage. Cohabitants with children will be entitled to Child Maintenance payments and can apply for financial assistance under Schedule 1 of the Children Act 1989.

▶ **Spousal benefits under a pension** – if your partner dies, their pension dies with them. They may have the opportunity to nominate you to receive certain benefits from their pension upon their death, but if you aren't married make sure you and your partner speak to the pension provider to ascertain what you can do to ensure that you benefit in the event of your partner's death, or vice versa.

▶ **Assets in someone else's name** – other than real estate, an unmarried person has no claim on assets in one person's sole name. So a policy, savings or investments are off limits unless they are in joint names. Any assets held in joint names (such as bank accounts or endowment policies) will be owned equally and will pass to the survivor in the event of the death of the other. For assets held in sole names (for example pensions or sole bank accounts) these remain your property and free from a claim by your cohabitant. Gifts will remain the property of the person who was given them. If you have joint debts then you will be jointly and severally liable for the debt. The debt company will not be concerned with who has had the benefit of the funds and, in the event of default on the loan, the creditor will pursue both of you as individuals for the full amount.

▶ **Real estate** – if you are not on the title deeds of a property, you do not gain a beneficial interest in a property just on the basis that you live there. If the person who owns the property asks you to leave, you have no right to stay in the property. In the absence of an express declaration in a deed or other document, a non-legal owner may acquire a beneficial interest by way of a constructive or resulting trust.

  ▶ A resulting trust can be found to exist by reference to the contributions made to the property, usually at the time of purchase. The contributions will nearly always result in a corresponding beneficial interest (so if you put in 60% of the purchase price and your partner the remaining 40%, you would be deemed to hold the beneficial interest in those shares).

  ▶ A constructive trust may be established if the non-legal owner has been promised an interest in the property by the legal owner, or there is some kind of "common intention" and they acted upon that promise to their detriment, e.g. they invested money in the property, such as building an extension. The common intention can be either at the time of purchase or subsequently. It is not necessary to have an explicit conversation about the beneficial ownership. The court can also look at the conduct of each of the parties.

Jointly owned property

One of the most common claims for professional negligence that the Solicitors' Regulatory Authority deal with are solicitors who fail to properly advise people who purchase property together on how to hold that property.

To help explain how all this works you may find the following definitions useful:

▶ "Equity" – the amount of money that would be realised if the property was sold. In short it can be calculated as follows: the value of the property less the mortgage and costs of sale (between 2% and 3% of the value of the property).

- ▶ "Beneficial Interest" – this is how the equity is held.

- ▶ "Legal Interest" – this is who is on the title deeds.

There are 3 options when deciding how to own a property jointly. These are:

1. **Joint Tenants** – this means that the owners of the property hold the entirety of the property, so if there are 2 owners you hold it 50:50, if there are 4 owners you hold a 25% share and so on. It further means that when one of the owners dies, their share passes to the remaining owners, e.g. 3 brothers own a property, one dies, the surviving 2 will see their share go from 33% to 50%. This is regardless of what the deceased may or may not have put in their will. So any purported gift of their share to someone else would fail. It is very easy to sever the tenancy: if you do sever the joint tenancy you will then hold the beneficial interest as Tenants in Common in equal shares. (see next point for an explanation of this).

2. **Tenants in Common in equal shares** – this does exactly what it says on the tin, you would hold the beneficial interest in equal shares. So, if there are 2 owners, you hold a distinct 50% of the equity. This means that upon your death, your specific share would go to whomever you name in your will.

3. **Tenants in Common in unequal shares** – this has the same effect as point 2, but instead of 50%, you would get whatever percentage you hold. As an example, you buy a property for £250,000 with your partner. You have a mortgage for £150,000, you pay £60,000 and your partner pays the balance towards the purchase price. You may want to consider holding the beneficial interest 60:40 in your favour. This means that when the property sells, you would receive 60% of the net proceeds of sale (i.e. the equity).

If you own a property jointly and have declared how you wish to own your beneficial interest then in the absence of fraud, mistake, or evidence of a subsequent agreement you will own the property in accordance with the declaration. If you have purchased your property after 1st April 1998 the transfer document (called a TR1) will contain an express declaration of your beneficial interests (provided you ticked the right box). You may also have signed a separate document, either at time of purchase or subsequently, called a deed of trust.

If, however, there is no express declaration of your beneficial interest, the starting point is to assume that you will be equally entitled to the equity. The Supreme Court has however decided that where it is not possible by direct evidence or inference to ascertain your intentions, they can decide your shares by looking at what they consider to be fair. Financial contributions are relevant but there are many other factors that the court may take into account.

If you currently own your property as joint tenants you can consider severing the joint tenancy. This can either be by agreement or unilaterally by serving notice on your co-owner. You can then enter into a living together agreement and have a will to specify where your interest will pass on your death.

Note of caution

If you fail to tick the right box on the TR1 form, you cannot do anything about it once the property has been purchased. So, for example, using the scenario above at number 3: if you ticked either box 1 or 2 you have just lost 10% of the equity and there is nothing you can do about it because you have an express declaration of trust saying you hold the beneficial interest equally.

CASE STUDY

A man buys a property with his girlfriend. He puts in £100,000 to the purchase price, and she puts in £5,000. They tick the "Joint Tenants" box on the TR1. They are deemed to hold the property jointly and equally. She has therefore just won the "property lottery". He then severs the joint tenancy, but by doing so he inadvertently creates a second declaration of trust that they own the property in equal shares, i.e. 50:50 – the final nail in the coffin that is his claim. Even if he hadn't severed the joint tenancy, the girlfriend would still be entitled to 50%, despite his much larger financial contribution to the purchase.

Considerations in the event of death

Cohabitants will not automatically inherit from one another under the rules of intestacy. Therefore the only way you can provide for a cohabitant on death is to make a will.

LAWYERS – FINDING THE RIGHT ONES AND WORKING WITH THEM

SUMMARY

Most people involved with family law issues consult a lawyer.

▶   If you engage a lawyer, you will probably have to sign an agreement, the terms of which determine your financial obligations to the lawyer.

▶   It is worth looking carefully at the agreement and understanding what you are going to be charged for and when you will be expected to pay.

▶   If you are not happy with your lawyer, you can change and, in some circumstances, you may consider making a formal complaint about their conduct.

▶   You can conduct your own family law matter – but whether you do is another matter.

Whether or not to engage a lawyer in a family law matter is often a question of cost (and whether you are prepared to set aside the time to do it yourself).

Remember to distinguish between legal advice and legal representation. You may need to obtain advice on the legal issues involved and how to deal with them, but still be able to represent yourself in negotiations and in the court process.

You can only do the analysis accurately if you understand both sides of the equation, the costs and the benefits. So here are some basic questions:

▶   How important (or complicated) are the issues?

▶   Am I able to do what needs to be done without legal advice or representation at all?

▸ How much legal advice do I need?

▸ Do I really need a lawyer to represent me?

▸ How much will this cost me?

▸ What additional costs or fees might I incur and what might they be for?

Another way to look at the cost-benefit analysis might be as follows:

Costs

▸ How much does my lawyer propose to charge me? What is the top and bottom of the range of costs that I will have to pay?

▸ Is the lawyer prepared to guarantee how much the costs will be before starting work?

▸ What results can the lawyer guarantee me for this outlay?

Benefits

▸ What legal advice do I need that I can't obtain myself by other means?

▸ When do I need this advice?

▸ What risks do I face if I don't have the advice?

▸ Will I know all the options available to me to move forward?

▸ Am I likely to get my matter resolved faster with a lawyer? Is the speed of resolution important for me?

▸ Do I know how to finalise my matter in a legal way?

▸ Is representation by a lawyer necessary in my case? If so, what benefits will this representation provide?

▸ What are the risks of not being represented?

▸ Am I likely to be overwhelmed by the work involved?

▸ Will it put me at a disadvantage if the other party is represented and I am not?

▸ Will the matter take a lot longer if I do it myself?

Most people who are involved in family law disputes would say that they are better off with a lawyer than without one. It's not much different to building a house. You are likely to be better off engaging a builder than doing it yourself.

When should I instruct a lawyer?

If you are thinking about separating or have recently separated, getting some sound legal advice is sensible. Initially, you may not even need a lawyer if there are no issues over children or property, although the cost of a preliminary meeting with a lawyer may be well worth the investment.

You are unlikely to be aware of your rights and responsibilities unless you have a pretty good knowledge of family law. Initially, you would only spend a minimal amount of money to get professional guidance about where you stand and the best way to move forward. Perhaps get a couple of legal opinions. You are not making a commitment to a long-term relationship with any lawyer at this stage; rather you are simply finding out the best way to handle the situation.

If you and your ex-partner have agreed the basic terms of your settlement, it makes sense to have a lawyer prepare the agreement in the proper legal form and get it lodged at court. Lawyers know what is required in the content of the agreement and the processes required for it to be formalised. They will also be able to tell you whether the proposed terms of settlement are fair and reasonable, or whether you are giving away too much.

At this stage, a lawyer should be able to provide a fairly accurate estimate (if not an actual and fixed quote) of what it will cost to prepare the requisite documents.

Time

It will probably be quicker if you have a lawyer to do the paperwork for a settlement. They know the processes and what has to be done to get matters finalised. A competent lawyer will know what to put in the agreement and what to leave out.

If in doubt, ask the lawyer how long it will take to finalise everything (get a commitment), and if you are not satisfied that everything will be handled promptly, go to another lawyer.

Certainty

All agreements over property should be in writing and formalised by a court in what is known as a Consent Order. Otherwise, your agreement is neither binding nor enforceable.

A lawyer can draft your agreement in the right terms and make sure that all of the loose ends are tied up, so that making the Consent Order will finalise your matter once and for all. This will give you the certainty that you won't have to deal with these issues again.

If you are attempting to do it yourself, there may be a nagging feeling that not everything has been ticked off (and anxiety about what the consequences of that failure might be).

Stress

Engaging a lawyer to draft up your settlement documents (and perhaps to negotiate any lingering unresolved issues) allow you to leave these worries in their hands. The lawyer will be able to resolve these matters objectively and in accordance with your instructions, relieving you of much of the stress you would otherwise face at this time.

Cost

If costs are reasonable and proportionate to the issues and the values involved, paying for a lawyer's skills is likely to be a realistic and fair investment for you. It might save a major court battle in the event matters are not properly dealt with in the first place, or finalised according to the law.

Again, it comes back to the question of what your lawyer proposes to charge for the services provided. You may find some lawyers are simply too expensive, as their hourly rates are comparatively high, relative to the job that you want them to do. At the end of the day, you are paying the money, so you must be satisfied that their services are worth it.

The cost of court proceedings can be very expensive. Anecdotal evidence suggests that the average case of fully contested proceedings at well in excess of £20,000 – for each party, not the combined cost! Some large cases take many years to work their way through the court system and can cost each side hundreds of thousands of pounds in legal fees.

Your decision to engage a lawyer has major financial consequences, so it is not to be taken lightly.

Most people whose matters end up in court do engage lawyers. There are some pretty obvious reasons for this:

- ▸ The court processes are complicated and demanding (lawyers are trained to deal with this).

- ▸ Appearing in court and presenting your own case is a daunting task — especially if the other party has a lawyer who knows the ropes.

- ▸ A lawyer can advise you about legally realistic alternatives.

- ▸ A lawyer can help you avoid the possible consequences of adverse Costs Orders.

The benefits of having competent representation and advice are pretty clear.

Insurance against bad lawyers

There is no guarantee that a lawyer will handle your matter competently and effectively. Despite the efforts of the regulatory bodies to ensure that lawyers maintain very high professional and ethical standards, there are bad apples in every barrel. If your lawyer makes a complete mess of your case, you may be able to take further action.

Firstly, you should follow the firm's internal complaints procedure. If you get no joy there you can lodge your complaint with the Legal Ombudsman. Complaints may be about overcharging, failure to follow instructions, improper conduct, etc. Your complaints will be investigated and your lawyer's handling of the matter examined.

You may be able to take action against your lawyer to recover any damages you may have incurred due to their failure to deal properly with your matter. For example, if your lawyer fails to draft appropriate orders to finalise your matter and you suffer losses as a result, the lawyer may be liable to you for damages as a result of their negligence.

Although obviously not a situation you would wish to be in, the chances of it happening are low and it might be better to take the risk than make a mess of your matter without a lawyer.

Choosing a lawyer

So, you have decided that it is probably in your best interests to have a lawyer. How do you find the right one?

In view of the importance of the issues at stake, this is a big decision and it is likely to have a significant impact on at least the next few months of your life.

Many people find their lawyer through the recommendation of a friend or colleague. Others use the Yellow Pages or contact the Law Society for a list of Family Law practitioners. If you do not have a direct recommendation, perhaps the best place to look is via Resolution, the umbrella organisation for the majority of family law solicitors nationwide. Solicitors who are members of Resolution are generally recognised as experts in their field and also have signed up to a Code of Conduct which is designed to reduce tension where possible and focus on the key issues involved in a matter.

If there are international issues that need to be considered, you should consider instructing a specialist family lawyer who is a member of the International Academy of Matrimonial Lawyers. Details of all members are available on their website.

Whichever method you choose, prepare a shortlist, then make appointments to talk to those on your list.

You should also determine up front whether you want to get matters resolved as quickly and cheaply as possible (but fairly for all parties), or whether you are spoiling for a fight, which might take a long time and cost a lot of money. No one can deny you your 'day in court', if that's what you are after. However, think about the consequences before you commit to that course of action. Whatever you decide will have a bearing on the kind of lawyer that you select.

Your first consultation with a lawyer does not mean that you are committed to that lawyer for the entire period of your case, or even at all. If you engage a lawyer and start working with them, you can pay the bill at any time and switch to another lawyer (or handle the matter yourself).

Specialist lawyers – there is a difference

In some areas of law – including Family Law – a number of lawyers with special knowledge and expertise are qualified as Accredited Specialists. A Family Law Accredited Specialist must be a lawyer who has a substantial Family Law practice, has passed intensive examination and skills testing, and maintains their professional qualifications by attending appropriate training each year. Each specialist has worked in Family Law for at least five years.

In a sense, a specialist in any area of law is similar to a specialist medical practitioner. If you have skin problems you would see a dermatologist, a paediatrician looks after children, if your eyes are playing up you might be referred to an ophthalmologist. So, if your legal issues are in relation to family law and you want some really expert advice, it makes sense to go to a specialist family lawyer.

Collaborative Law

Collaborative law is a model originally developed in the USA about 20 years ago. It is also available in Canada, Australia and New Zealand, as well in the UK. It is offered by a number of different Family Law solicitors, although not all. Check with Resolution to find a local lawyer trained in the Collaborative Law process.

What is Collaborative Law?

In recent years, a growing number of lawyers have been practising 'collaborative law' nationwide. This is a negotiation model where lawyers and their clients sign an agreement to work together to resolve a dispute without court involvement. The stated aim is to reach agreement while minimising costs, delays and stress.

Theoretically, this process aligns your lawyer's interests with yours as the client, as both you and your lawyer want to get the dispute settled.

If required, financial advisors, accountants or valuers may also be brought into the negotiations.

Under collaborative law, lawyers must cease their involvement if the negotiations fail to produce an agreement; they are not permitted to act for their clients in any later court process. If the process is unsuccessful, both sides must find new lawyers and start from scratch – and this would come at a financial and time cost.

Under collaborative law, the discussions and negotiations are 'without prejudice' – that is, private discussions where nothing said or conceded can be used later in evidence.

Features of the collaborative process

Some lawyers who practice collaborative law claim that it achieves a win-win outcome and that it allows you to:

> ▸ Maintain control of the process, as well as preserving privacy and dignity.

> ▸ Participate in a structured and interest-based negotiation, and

> ▸ Have an open and transparent exchange of all information.

If you are thinking of using the process, consider how realistic these claims are and whether these benefits are likely to occur, or whether they are really to be expected of any lawyer committed to acting in your best interests, regardless of the process followed.

Questions at your first meeting with a lawyer

When you first meet a lawyer, ask as many questions as necessary to assess whether that person is likely to be the right lawyer for you. After all, the relationship might last for many months, sometimes years. You need to have confidence in the lawyer's abilities and competence, and be comfortable about working with them for the long haul.

Think about what you want from your lawyer before you meet them. What things are important to you? Are you looking for a lawyer who is likely to:

> ▸ Conduct matters in a constructive and non-confrontational way?

> ▸ Retain professional objectivity?

> ▸ Consider the long-term consequences of actions and communications?

> ▸ Encourage clients to put the interests of the children first?

> ▸ Stress the importance of being open and honest?

- ▶ Encourage all parties to behave in a civilised way?

- ▶ Keep financial issues separate to children's matters?

- ▶ Be up front on costs issues; how much you are expected to pay, when and how?

- ▶ Balance the benefits of any steps against the likely costs (financial and emotional) and maintain a sense of proportionality about your costs?

- ▶ Inform you of all your options: counselling, family therapy, round-table negotiations, mediation and court proceedings?

- ▶ Work pro-actively on your matter and focus on results, not the time they spend?

- ▶ Keep you informed about progress in your matter and relevant dates?

When you meet a family lawyer, ask about these issues and how they approach family law. Try also to get a sense of the lawyer's knowledge and skills. You should ask:

- ▶ How much will it cost?

- ▶ How long will it take?

- ▶ What is the lawyer's experience in family law?

- ▶ What are your options?

- ▶ What is the best plan for your matter?

Work out some realistic and achievable objectives. There is no point starting off with totally unachievable expectations. That's like selecting an estate agent just because he says he can sell your house for the highest price, regardless of the state of the market.

Assess your lawyer's negotiating skills. Have you found someone who is a listener and prepared to consider all points of view? Or are they dogmatic and opinionated?

If your matter involves complex issues, make sure your lawyer is skilled and experienced in the relevant areas and has dealt before with similar matters.

Always ask the lawyer how they intend to approach your matter; in particular, what's the action plan, how will it be achieved and in approximately what time frame? You want to hire someone who is committed to obtaining achievable and realistic results. It is pretty meaningless to ask a lawyer about their 'success rates'. Family law is more about a fair division rather than a win-lose approach. You would be better off to ask them about their settlement rate: how many of their matters get resolved and within what period of time? Lawyers who talk about family law in win-lose terms might be more inclined to create drawn-out confrontations in court, rather than find sensible and reasonable solutions for all parties.

Some lawyers are very busy and may not be able to give your matter the kind of attention it requires. Be wary of those who simply want to pass your matter on to a more junior, or less experienced lawyer. It is in your interests to have well-qualified lawyers doing complex legal work, but you may not want to carry the cost of a more accomplished lawyer for the less difficult paperwork involved in a family law matter. There is a balance.

By now, you will have a good impression whether the lawyers you have spoken to have identified the relevant issues in your particular matter and are capable of providing you with sound advice about the issues and your options.

However, at the end of your conversation, you need to assess whether you can relate to that person and whether they relate to you. You're not looking for a new best friend, but you are looking for someone to discuss your family law issues with honestly and openly.

What your lawyer will want to know

When you go to your first meeting with a lawyer, it really helps if you are prepared and have all of the relevant information available to you.

First, be as clear as possible about the reasons for consulting a lawyer. This sets the tone for your meeting and will enable your lawyer to put the response in context. Are you, for example, seeking general guidance about family law and how it might apply in your case, or are you responding to proceedings that may have commenced or seeking advice on proceedings that you want to start.

Secondly, have all the information available that may assist the lawyer, such as financial documents, bank statements and mortgage balances. The more you have, the easier and quicker it will be for the lawyer. Prepare a schedule of your assets and liabilities (as best known to you). If you do not know what bank and credit card accounts you and your partner have, bring any information that is at hand that may assist in tracing those details, such as the names of banks that have been used or details of your ex-partner's employment. But under no circumstances take your ex-partner's documents with you, unless you are named on the property or account.

Thirdly, answer all of the lawyer's questions honestly and fully and do not withhold any information that you think might not be of assistance in your matter. If your lawyer is not told the full position, it is unlikely that the advice you receive will be of full value and may, indeed, be incorrect.

Lastly, tell the lawyer exactly what you want to achieve. What you want may not be achievable but you should give the lawyer an opportunity to consider the possibilities and not guess what you are seeking. Lawyers are not mind readers. If you are not sure what you want, say so.

Objectivity in Family Law matters

Beware of the lawyer who appears to be more than simply compassionate and understanding – the one who starts to identify with the issues and the individuals, who treats the other side as the 'enemy' and who sees family law as a battleground.

It's always nice to have someone who is sympathetic to your issues and understands how tough it is for you. However, there is a danger that a lawyer who becomes overly involved in your matter and starts to identify with it may lose objectivity, to the detriment of your best interests.

There are many stories about how family law clients end up paying large sums just to have a lawyer listen patiently to their every problem. Time is money (your money), so use a lawyer to help with your legal problems, not your emotional ones. Your lawyer's job is:

▸ To make an objective assessment and advise you on your legal situation.

▸ To tell you what your options are, and which might be, most appropriate to pursue, and

▸ To take your instructions and conduct matters with skill and professionalism.

They are not a shoulder for you to cry on. However, if you are finding the emotional fallout from separation difficult, your lawyer should be able to recommend counselling and support services available to you.

After the first meeting

Following your meeting with a prospective lawyer, you should ask for a written initial advice and a case plan setting out how your matter will be conducted, with time and cost estimates. This does not have to be in great detail but should set out the main points of your matter, the advice you have received, the options and proposals to move on, and the anticipated costs.

From these documents, you should learn what your lawyer proposes to do in order to deal with your issues, including:

▸ The lawyer's understanding of the relevant information that he or she has received from you.

▸ The lawyer's legal and strategic advice based on that information.

▸ The lawyer's understanding of your instructions on how to proceed, and

▸ Where the matter should progress to from here.

An indication of the lawyer's efficiency is how much time passes before you receive this information. If the lawyer tells you that, due to workload, the information cannot be provided in less than a couple of weeks, move on.

Remember that the lawyer you select will work with you on matters that are probably going to have an impact on you and your family for the rest of your life. So, it is vital that you make a really informed decision to maximise your chances of making the right one.

Working with your lawyer

Your relationship with your lawyer is governed by professional ethical standards set out by the relevant SRA and by the engagement letter you both sign.

However, never forget that you are in charge. You are paying the bills and you are the one who gives the final instructions. Your lawyer can advise and push you in whatever direction they might think is appropriate, but you always call the shots. For example, if you want to settle and your lawyer wants to fight, simply give the order "settle" and the lawyer must do all in their power to get the matter resolved.

Having said that, there are certain ground rules that apply to your relationship with your lawyer.

Your responsibilities

The Agreement

Read the terms and conditions carefully to ensure that you know what your obligations are: financial and otherwise.

Disclosure and honesty - You must be honest and disclose all facts and information that might be relevant to your matter. If you do not do so, your lawyer cannot be held responsible for any negative consequences that might follow. For example, if you fail to disclose that you have a bank account overseas, or a drug problem that might impact on your capacity to look after your children, and these facts are brought up later, you are unlikely to be seen positively by the court.

Response to requests - You should respond promptly to all requests from your lawyer for information or documents that might be required in court proceedings. If the lawyer cannot prepare for a court hearing or file documents that are required because you have not provided them, you may face a costs order for not being ready to proceed. The lawyer cannot be blamed for that.

Pay your bills - You should pay all the bills the lawyer sends you in accordance with your Agreement. If you have a query about what you have been charged, raise it straight away. If you have problems paying your bills, tell the lawyer so that alternative arrangements might be made. A lawyer is entitled to stop working on your matter if you do not meet your financial obligations, which could leave you in a difficult situation.

Your lawyer's responsibilities

Professionalism and care - Your lawyer has a duty of care to you. They have an obligation to work diligently and professionally on your matter and you should be advised of anything that affects that responsibility. For example, you must be advised if your lawyer is ill and unable to attend to the requirements of your case. If your lawyer cannot attend court because of prior commitments, you should be told.

Part of your lawyer's duty is to ensure that you are kept informed about relevant dates and deadlines; for example, when you have to attend court, or sign documents. Your lawyer should always keep ahead in the planning of your case and keep you advised of what is going on.

Obviously your lawyer has a responsibility to advise you accurately about the law and about your rights and responsibilities under that law. This advice should be specific and sufficiently detailed so that you understand which laws apply and what the effect of those laws is on your case. For example:

> If you have received a significant inheritance immediately prior to your separation, your lawyer should advise how the relevant law will affect your entitlement to keep the proceeds of this inheritance.

> If you intend to take your children to live with you overseas, your lawyer should make you aware of the impact of such a decision.

Copies of correspondence and documents - Your lawyer should keep you advised of all relevant communications, such as letters to and from the other party, copies of court documents and orders of the court. These should be sent to you very soon after they have been sent or received, not months later.

Confirm instructions - Your lawyer should always seek or confirm your instructions about running your matter. They must ask for your instructions about offers to settle, or possible court orders that might be made by consent. Don't forget that you are in charge and your lawyer must get your instructions on the major decisions.

Not happy with your lawyer?

You may have legitimate cause for complaint about your lawyer. Your complaints might be about over-charging and legal costs, your lawyer's level of competence, their failure to keep you properly informed, unprofessional conduct (such as not telling you the correct information about your case), a general lack of organisation and inability to manage your case, or a refusal to communicate properly (for example, persistently failing to return your calls and correspondence).

If so, you can move on

Firstly, lay your cards on the table and speak to your lawyer. There is no point in just grumbling about the situation or feeling that you are not getting value for the fees you are paying. If your lawyer does not provide satisfactory answers to your concerns, you can always change lawyers. You can ask to be transferred to another lawyer within the same firm, or ask for a final account, pay it and take your files to someone else. However, consider carefully before taking this action; your new lawyer will have to learn everything about your file in order to represent you properly and there may be a significant cost involved in the process.

Always check how much your new lawyer intends to charge you for this refresher, as it may be quite costly if the matter has been going for a while. These costs may be justified where your current lawyer is not achieving timely results or shows incompetence in handling your matter.

Complaints about costs

Sometimes the bills you receive can give rise to a complaint.

This can be a difficult area, as payment on the basis of hourly rates can be pretty open-ended. Hourly rates are often criticised because they tend to reward the slower and less competent lawyers. Just because one lawyer's hourly rate is lower than the next does not guarantee that your total fees will be less. In fact, they may be a whole lot more.

Challenging an account means that your lawyer should have to provide evidence of the time spent on your matter. However, the outcome is often unpredictable, as the test is whether the work undertaken was necessary and the time taken was reasonable.

If you do not get reasonable satisfaction from your lawyer about a costs complaint, you can take the matter further and make a formal complaint to the Legal Ombudsman or, in extreme cases, the courts to have your bill independently assessed.

Doing it yourself

No family lawyer can guarantee you the result that you want. No lawyer can promise you that the matter will not go to court. However, if having a lawyer saves you time, gets your issues resolved legally and comes at a reasonable cost, you may decide that this advice and representation really is worthwhile. If not, you should do it yourself.

If you do your own case, you will have to do all the work that would normally be done by a lawyer, from beginning to end. This includes preparing documents, filing them in court, communications with the other party and generally keeping the case moving.

You will also have to be your own barrister and appear for yourself in preliminary negotiations, hearings in court and in conferences and meetings to discuss the matter.

Can you do it yourself?

Yes and it won't cost anything, as you don't charge yourself legal fees. Nothing prevents anyone from being their own lawyer, drafting up their own documents, complying with the court's requirements and representing themselves in court.

However, it is a very time-consuming process and there are pitfalls. For a start, you may be too close to the issues and this may affect your objectivity. It is very difficult to disassociate yourself from the rights and wrongs, especially if you are one of the parties involved.

The processes involved in 'running' a children's or property case are well known to a family lawyer. This does not mean that you cannot learn them, but it will take time and you may make many mistakes.

You will have to do all your own preparation and documentation, you may have to interview witnesses and prepare court documents for your witnesses and you will certainly have to gather all of the evidence that may be relevant to your matter and present it in the best possible light.

At the Final Hearing, you will also have to deal with the evidence of the other side and cross-examine your ex-partner.

BARRISTERS — WHO THEY ARE AND WHAT THEY DO

Barristers are lawyers who have decided to focus on the specific legal task of representing clients in court proceedings and advise on complex legal issues. They may also run mediations and do other tasks. However, their main focus is turning up in court to argue cases.

Your lawyer may represent you at interim hearings in court, where the issues are short and often procedural but, when you get to the Final Hearing stage, your lawyer is likely to suggest taking on a barrister to represent you.

Why hire a barrister? Why not have your lawyer stand up and speak for you throughout the Final Hearing? After all, they've got you this far.

Hiring a barrister is usually a good idea for the Final Hearing and for more complex hearings. This is because a good barrister:

> ▸ Will be an excellent public speaker, trained to be convincing, clear and argue well.

> ▸ Will have an excellent working knowledge of the law, particularly the laws relating to evidence, i.e. what may, and may not, be said in court.

> ▸ Will be trained to examine and cross-examine witnesses and have considerable experience in this art (it's harder than it looks on TV!).

> ▸ Will be aware of the workings of the rules of the court and will know when to object if the other side is doing something inappropriate, and

> ▸ Will be adept at the art of directing the discussion. They will encourage the judge to focus on things that are good for your case, while brushing over the things that perhaps do not make you look so good.

Of course, not all barristers have all of these skills to the same high level, but a good barrister will be able to do all of these things.

Presenting your case at a Final Hearing is not what you see on LA Law or Judge Judy. If you don't have at least a basic understanding of the rules of evidence and court procedures, you may find yourself at a significant disadvantage; especially if the other party has legal representation. Good barristers are not only clever with words and quick on their feet, they are usually very knowledgeable about the rules and know what can and can't be put to the court.

They are also aware of the nuances of the case as it progresses. They know when to shift their position to counter the other party's arguments as they emerge. They also have the ability to exploit weaknesses through cross-examination.

THE ELEPHANT IN THE ROOM – LEGAL COSTS

SUMMARY

▶   Legal fees in Family Law matters can be expensive.

▶   You don't only have to pay for your solicitor's time – you will also have to pay for the expenses that your solicitor accrues on your behalf (hiring experts to value your house, engaging a barrister) and court fees.

▶   Matrimonial and Child Law is not the kind of law where the loser pays. Instead, unless there are unusual circumstances, each person pays their own costs. Even if you get what you want in the end, you will still have to pay your lawyer. The exception to this rule is in unmarried property disputes.

▶   The legal fees you pay may end up being more expensive than the difference you are arguing over. It may come down to a question of whether you would rather give the money to a lawyer or share it with your ex.

▶   It is very difficult to get free legal advice or support. Legal Aid is only available in very limited circumstances.

▶   Most family lawyers charge by the hour, some firms may offer fixed fee plans for your family law matter.

Let's Talk about The Money

It will come as no surprise to hear that legal costs can be very high.

Reports of family law cases where the legal fees cost each party tens and sometimes hundreds of thousands of pounds are not uncommon. On the other hand, many matters also resolve quickly and without great expense.

Apart from the media, no one seems to like talking about legal costs. Lawyers can be unhelpful and vague about likely future fees and clients often don't want to hear about them anyway. Legal costs are 'the elephant in the room': the subject that everyone pretends is not there in the vain hope that the problem will go away. However, the issue does not go away, so it may as well be addressed fully at the first opportunity.

Different fee arrangements

By far the most common fee arrangement is to pay by way of the lawyer's hourly rate. You should think of your fees being like a taxi-meter running. Most lawyers will bill regularly and most will expect their invoices to be paid within a month.

Some solicitors will offer a fixed fee, although this isn't anywhere near as common as payment on an hourly rate.

Time-based fees

Time-based fees are when you are charged on the basis of the time spent by your lawyer. Your lawyer's 'hourly rate' (how much they charge for each hour of work they perform) is multiplied by the amount of time they spend on your matter to arrive at the amount you have to pay.

Fixed fees

Fixed fees are arrangements you have with your lawyer before any work begins, about what will be charged for undertaking the agreed work.

Which fee method to choose

There may be advantages and disadvantages in each of the fee arrangements.

Hopefully, the difficulties of comparing the different arrangements – a bit like trying to compare apples with oranges – may become clearer as you read the rest of this chapter.

Questions to ask about legal costs in Family Law

Apart from the question about which fee arrangement might apply to your case, there are several vital issues you should understand about legal costs in family law:

- ▸   What are you paying for?

- ▸   How much will it cost you?

- ▸   Who pays the costs?

- ▸   When are they paid?

- ▸   How are they paid?

You should make sure you are clear on the answers to these questions before engaging your lawyer.

What are you paying for?

Depending on which fee arrangement applies in your case, you will normally have to pay for:

- ▸   Your lawyer's time

- ▸   Your lawyer's disbursements (expenses and payments made on your behalf such as court fees, expert's fees and barrister's fees), and

- ▸   VAT.

Your lawyer's time

It is really important for anyone who proposes to use a lawyer to know how a lawyer charges fees and how they calculate their bills. After all, you are the one who has to pay them.

Most lawyers who work in family law will charge you according to the amount of time they spend on your matter. The lawyer should have an agreement with you setting out what the rates are. This is known as an engagement letter and should set out how the lawyer is to be retained.

The actual fee charged is calculated by multiplying the lawyer's hourly rate by the amount of time spent working on your matter. If a lawyer has an hourly rate of £250 and spends 10 hours working on your matter, you will be charged £2,500. If you had a lawyer with an hourly rate of £400, your bill for the same hours of work would be £4,000. There will be VAT on top of this, plus the cost of any disbursements (e.g. fees for a barrister). The bills are simply a measure of the amount of time your lawyer has spent working on your case – regardless of the result.

So, when you go to see a lawyer who tells you that their hourly rate is £250 plus VAT, they are not telling you how much the matter will cost, they are just telling you what you have to pay for every hour of their time.

Lawyers are obliged to give you an estimate of what your overall costs will be, but an estimate is exactly that. Most of these estimates will have a large range between the upper and lower figure as it can be difficult to estimate what a matter will cost over the whole journey. In short, it's a bit like asking how long is a piece of string?

Different hourly rates do not necessarily assist in working out how big or small your bill will be. A lawyer charging £300 an hour might be an absolute whizz and do a particular job in much less time than a less experienced (but still competent) lawyer who charges, say, £160 an hour. Different hourly rates may help you to assess a lawyer's relative experience (and expense), but this knowledge does not enable you to calculate what your legal costs will be at the end of the day. You might actually spend a lot less with a lawyer who has a higher hourly rate.

What is included in time?

Although most lawyers charge by the time they spend on your matter, it is important to know what is included in 'chargeable time' and what is not. As a rule, they charge for work that is 'necessary' and 'reasonable' and that furthers your case. This could include:

▶ Attending meetings and conferences.

▶ Taking instructions from you.

▶ Taking evidence from people involved in your case.

▶ Preparing before meetings, or preparing notes afterwards.

▶ Considering (thinking about) and researching issues to do with your matter.

▶ Discussing your matter on the telephone (with you or anyone else).

▶ Preparing and sending letters, faxes and/or emails (to you or anyone else).

- ▶ Reading and considering letters, faxes and/or emails (from you or anyone else).

- ▶ Copying letters, faxes and/or emails to you or others who might be involved in your case.

- ▶ Looking at documents provided by you or by others and taking copies or making notes about those documents.

- ▶ Preparing documents for court or for hearings.

- ▶ Attending hearings in court.

- ▶ Meeting with a barrister to discuss your matter or preparing documents for the barrister.

- ▶ Waiting for a hearing to start in court, or a conference.

- ▶ Travelling to and from the court, and

- ▶ Discussing your matter with someone else (personally or on the telephone).

Whatever time your lawyer spends on these activities will be charged to you.

How to keep costs down

Practical points to consider in ensuring that your lawyer's time is not increased unnecessarily, and where you can help, include the following:

- ▶ Use telephone conversations to discuss only relevant legal issues. Don't use telephone calls as an opportunity to complain about your ex-partner – it can be very expensive.

- ▶ Prepare for telephone calls or meetings in advance with a list of questions so you will be focused upon the issues you want to cover.

- ▶ Collect documentation yourself and ensure that it is given to your lawyer in a clear and orderly manner so that it reduces the time they will spend on considering your documents.

- ▶ Try and keep email correspondence to a minimum. A high level of email correspondence is often the reason for increased legal costs. Lawyers will charge for all emails sent and received.

Fixed fees in Family Law

Fixed fees are pretty simple. You and your lawyer discuss a plan for your matter, the work required to execute that plan and the amount to be paid for that work. You then discuss how you will pay for the agreed costs. If you reach agreement, you sign a contract and the lawyer gets working.

Fixed fees may not be appropriate for all cases. For example, where complex and uncertain legal issues need to be resolved, a fixed fee may not be offered to you.

Advantages of fixed fees

The advantages of a fixed fee arrangement in your family law matter are pretty straightforward:

▸   You know up front exactly what your costs will be.

▸   You can make realistic arrangements about how and when to pay your legal bills, and

▸   You will pay a fee that equals the value you and your lawyer place on the work to be done, not the time it may take.

Comparing fixed fees with hourly rates – apples and oranges

Can you compare a fixed fee arrangement with the initial estimates that are given where an hourly rate is being used? Unfortunately not. They are totally different practices and are based on entirely different principles.

With fixed fees: you know what you are getting yourself into before you start the engagement and, therefore, you have certainty about the price you will pay. But if you settle much earlier than the lawyer envisaged, you may find you've overpaid for the work.

With hourly rates: you can only know after the engagement what you have to pay. You get an estimate (which may or may not turn out to be accurate). The cost will be determined by the amount of time your lawyer takes to complete your matter.

Disbursements

You are also required to pay 'disbursements'. These are expenses incurred on your behalf, other than the fees you pay for your lawyer's time. These costs are payable by you if you are being charged on a time billing arrangement and may or may not be included in a fixed fee agreement.

Typically, these costs include:

- ▸ Fees charged for work done by other professionals (for example, barristers, actuaries, valuers, psychologists).

- ▸ Costs incurred while managing a matter, such as courier fees, and

- ▸ 'Soft' disbursements, such as photocopying.

The cost of barristers

If your lawyer wishes to engage a barrister to represent you in court, or to obtain an opinion about your matter, you should ask why this is necessary and what the likely costs will be. Barristers usually charge a fixed fee for hearings, but can also charge by the hour, more usually for conferences. Your solicitor should agree before the hearing what the barrister will be charging for the hearing and they will invariably ask you to pay the fees up front, before the hearing takes place. If your hearing is listed for a period of more than a day, the barrister will charge a "Brief Fee" for preparation of the hearing and attending the first day, then a "Refresher Fee" (which is generally less than the brief fee) for every subsequent day of the hearing.

Court fees and charges

Court fees are also described as a disbursement – a cost you will have to pay. The fees for filing documents in court and for hearings are all set out on the following website, www.justice.gov.uk/courts/fees. These are almost always paid before the event or when filing documents.

You may qualify for a reduction in fees in some instances, so it is worth checking whether or not this is the case with the courts.

So, how much will my matter cost?

The actual cost of each matter will depend upon a range of factors including:

- ▸ The fee arrangement you choose.
- ▸ The complexity of your matter.
- ▸ The efficiency and effectiveness of your legal representation, and
- ▸ How quickly you can get the matter resolved.

Where any of these factors is unknown, it is difficult to work out precisely what your fees will be. That is why lower and upper ranges may vary widely.

Ranges of fees

In family law matters where you are being charged according to the time spent on your case, your lawyer should give you an estimate of how much it will cost to do the work you require. However, these estimates are not the final word and your bill may exceed the original estimate by a significant amount. That is not necessarily the lawyer's fault as matters can develop in unexpected ways. However, the bigger the estimated range, the more careful you should be. Ask the lawyer to talk you through the estimate and explain the ranges given.

The extent of the range may reflect the fact that there are significant unknowns in your case.

A lawyer is required to update you with details about your fees on a regular basis and you are always entitled to ask for their estimates of future costs and likely disbursements.

Your best chance of minimising the overall costs (and keeping them at the lower end of the estimated range) is to get the matter settled as early as possible. This is because with time billing, the longer it goes on, the more hours that the lawyer puts in, meaning that it is more likely the upper limits of the estimated range will be tested.

With fixed fees, you will know how much you have to pay at each stage of the work that is required and estimates are likely to be given only for work in the future that may or may not be required.

Who pays the costs in family law matters?

Family law is not a 'loser pays' jurisdiction, unlike most other civil jurisdictions. In the Family Courts, each party invariably pays their own costs.

In certain circumstances you can apply for an interim order for your ex-spouse to pay an interim lump sum that you then use towards your legal fees. See Interim Spousal Maintenance in Chapter 1 and refer to sections 22ZA and 22ZB of the Matrimonial Causes Act.

Again (although this is not an absolute rule) it is safe to assume you will have to pay your own legal costs in the vast majority of cases. Therefore, you must carefully consider the costs you will incur and the financial impact of running a legal case.

Costs Orders

A costs order is where one party has to pay some (and in some circumstances, all) of the other person's legal costs. Costs orders may be made against the other party in situations where they have failed to adhere to the court timetable and/or failed to disclose all their financial disclosure.

Proportionality

Try to keep a sense of proportion between the likely cost of your matter and the potential outcome of taking a matter to court. In other words, weigh up what you are arguing about against the likely costs of that argument. This is a less difficult task where the argument is about property.

Take a simple example:

▸   You have total property worth £250,000 (after deducting all your debts).

▸   You want a 60:40 split in your favour (£150,000 for you).

▸   Your ex-partner wants a 50:50 split (£125,000 for you), and

▸   You are therefore 10 per cent apart (£25,000).

Each party's lawyer estimates that taking it to court will cost £30,000

> ▸   If you win, you end up with £120,000 (£150,000, less £30,000 costs).

> ▸   If you lose, you end up with £95,000 (£125,000, less £30,000 costs).

You could have compromised at the start for the amount that the other person was offering and been better off. That is a true lose-lose outcome.

Therefore, it often makes sense to look for a compromise solution that does not expose everyone to potentially crippling legal costs.

So negotiate, mediate and wherever possible, settle. Do whatever it takes to come to reasonable agreements.

When must fees be paid?

Like everyone in business, your lawyer must be paid. How and when you must make the payments is a vital discussion that you must have with your lawyer at the earliest possible moment.

Unless you are on a fixed fee, you can usually expect to receive a bill from your lawyer at the end of each month. It will set out what work has been done and how much you have to pay.

With fixed fees, you would normally receive your bill after each quoted stage of the work has been completed.

The payment options will depend entirely on the agreement you have reached with your lawyer.

Monthly Payments

In most circumstances, your lawyer will expect you to pay your account in full each month from whatever sources might be available to you. Most lawyers expect payment within 30 days of the bill being issued and may stop working on your matter if the money does not arrive by then.

Up-front payments

Some lawyers will want you to pay into their Client Account a fixed sum of money, or an amount equal to their estimate for the total amount of work, before they even start work.

THE CLIENT ACCOUNT

Money on trust

Payment 'on account' into a lawyer's Client Account before starting work on your matter is not unusual.

You are providing the lawyer with the best kind of security that they will be paid after their services have been delivered, particularly where you are paying an open-ended hourly rate. When you put your money into the lawyer's Client Account, it remains there until drawn down to pay their fees and costs as they are billed.

Covering disbursements

Almost all lawyers require you to pay some money into their Client Account to cover them for 'disbursements' they are likely to incur. For example, if a court hearing is coming up and a barrister has been briefed, the lawyer will ask you for the full amount of the barrister's costs to be paid into their Client Account before the barrister starts work. Similarly, if a valuation is required, your lawyer will want the cost of that valuation paid into the Client Account so they can pay the valuer as soon as the report is provided.

Pay-at-the-end (PATE)

Whether time billing or fixed fees, some lawyers will allow you to pay your fees at the end of the matter (and may charge you interest). In these circumstances, the lawyer will want some form of security for the payment, such as a mortgage over property or a guarantee from a third party. If the lawyer is 'carrying' you in this way (effectively being a bank by lending you the money), it is not unreasonable that they should want these securities or that they should charge interest.

How are you going to pay your legal costs?

Whether you are paying up front, each month or at the end of your matter, it is pointless engaging lawyers if you are unable or unwilling to pay for their services.

Legal fees have to be paid – whether from your wages, a draw-down on investments, sale of a property or a business or shares, from savings or borrowings through a credit card, personal loan, overdraft or money lent to you by a relative or friend. So, at the time you decide to engage a lawyer, you should discuss exactly how the payment would be made.

Legal Aid and free services

There is now very little financial assistance available for a family law case.

You may find local legal services that provide pro-bono (free) assistance – but this is likely to be available only in limited circumstances and if you are in a very difficult financial position. You can also ask a lawyer if they are prepared to take on your case on a pro-bono basis. It is an unlikely outcome, but you may be lucky.

If you cannot afford a lawyer at all but you need legal assistance, you may be eligible for public funding (known as Legal Aid), but the availability of this was severely restricted from April 2013.

Legal funding loans

Another option is to seek a loan from a third party, generally a litigation funding company that provides you with the funds to meet your legal expenses.

This will come at a cost and you will need to bear the following points in mind:

▸ Fees will be payable to establish the loan and interest will be charged.

▸ The lender may require security over a property in which you have an interest (to ensure that there is a source of payment if you cannot repay the loan at the end of the matter).

▸ Usually you repay all of the loan plus the fees and interest after all of the proceedings have been finalised, and

▸ If you do not repay whatever is owing, the security may be sold to pay the loan and the costs of enforcing the loan agreement.

Other credit arrangements for legal fees

Using a credit card or arranging a loan facility from your bank are also options for the payment of legal fees.

If you are unable to negotiate an early settlement, you may have to approach relatives and friends to assist you with payment of your legal fees. In such circumstances a formal loan agreement will need to be put in place and interest will need to be paid on the loan.

Where you have to borrow money to pay fees, this may be taken into account in the final property distribution. However, it is only a likely scenario where the other party has the means to pay their legal costs and, without the loan, you do not.

MYTHS AND REALITY IN FAMILY LAW

Over time, many myths have grown around family law. We all know someone who has been involved in family disputes and they all have a horror story to tell – many get much better in the telling.

The particular laws that apply in this area are updated and changed quite frequently and this can lead to misunderstandings about what happens when couples separate. Recent changes have added to these misunderstandings.

Media reports often focus on sensationalist aspects of family law cases; for example, headlines such as 'Mistress claims assets', or 'Family Court awards father equal time' can create even further misconceptions in the public mind.

What follows are some examples of common misunderstandings and the reality.

Fault at separation

"If the separation is one person's 'fault' for example, because they had an affair or abandoned the family) they will be punished and the other person may get more of the property or more time with the children."

It doesn't work that way, as unfair as it may seem. Family law in England and Wales looks primarily to the future: what will you need in the future (financially) and what arrangements can be made for your children that are in their best interests. Although you may be hurt by the actions of your ex, there are no legal provisions to 'punish' them by giving you more in the division of money or time with children.

Common law spouse

"I've lived with my boyfriend for 6 months, surely I'm entitled to something?"

There is no such thing as a common law wife/husband. You can live with someone for 50 years, but if you aren't married you aren't entitled to anything upon separation as of right. You may be able to establish a beneficial interest in a property, but this is a very complex area of law and would require you to obtain legal advice to see if you fall into this category.

Custody of pets

"We can get orders in court to both have time (or 'share custody' in the American phrasing) with our dog/cat/goldfish."

'Fluffy' may be part of your family but the law sees pets as property, not as people. After all, Fluffy can't say whom she wants to live with anyway!

Property is divided between the two people involved; legally, your pet will belong to one or the other of you after separation, and orders will not be made for you to 'share time' with the pet.

Of course, you can come to an arrangement between yourselves about time sharing with your pet and carry it out yourselves. However, if there is an argument between you about time with the pet, the only way a court can solve it is by allocating the pet to one of you, solely as part of the property division.

Listening to kids

"The kids have said they only want to live with me and they don't want to see their Dad/ Mum. The court has to listen to them, right?"

This depends on the age of your children. If they are not teenagers, other considerations will probably carry more weight. If the children are older and show maturity, the court will give more weight to their opinions. Especially as children reach the age of 13 or 14, it is difficult to force them to spend time with a parent they do not want to spend time with.

The family courts are very good at assessing whether an opinion is a child's own opinion or something that their parent has talked them into saying. If you try to influence your children's views and this becomes known, the Judge will not think much of your abilities as a parent. If there is any question about what your children really think and why, the court may have a CAFCASS officer speak to them alone, find out what they think and report back to the court.

It's against Dads

"Family Law is prejudiced against Dads. Mum will automatically get more time with the children if the case goes to court."

This is not true; however there are reasons why it may seem to be.

Studies have shown that young children (under the age of five or six) need the stability of living consistently with one parent. Sharing that involves different evenings in different places is not necessarily in their best interests. However, it is good for children to have frequent time with the other parent to maintain their relationship.

When they are at school age, children cope much better with time sharing between parents and more equal time-sharing arrangements might be appropriate.

It may seem unfair that one parent gets more time with younger children than the other, but don't forget that the law prioritises children's best interests over parents' best interests.

The best position on separation

"Now that we're separated, my ex will be able to take all my money because the kids mostly live with her."

OR

"Now that we're separated, my ex will get to keep all the money because he's the breadwinner and I won't be able to support the kids."

Neither of these is true.

Nobody will get to keep "all the money": not you and not your ex either. Instead, the law tries to ensure that both are financially supported, with the amount and method of support depending on the circumstances in each case.

Provision for the kids through Child Support can be sorted out in a number of ways. If you are worried that your partner used to support you financially and now you don't have any source of income, you may want to investigate applying for spousal maintenance (but only if you are married).

Allegations of abuse

"If a mother makes allegations of abuse against a father, she will be believed and he will be punished by not being allowed to see his children."

The Family Courts are very good at assessing the difference between real and false allegations of abuse.

The court will look at what is said by witnesses in court, as well as evidence such as police records, doctors' and hospital records, reports from schools and from social services.

The court looks very critically upon people who make up allegations of abuse. It may even order you to pay some or all of the costs of the other person.

Even if allegations of abuse are found to be true, they don't necessarily mean that the abusive parent will be prevented from seeing their children, although an independent person may supervise visits to make sure nothing goes wrong.

What are assets?

"Compensation payments, inheritances and gifts are never included as assets to be distributed if you separate."

Compensation, damages awards and inheritances will normally be included in the marital pot, if they are in existence at the date of reckoning. But inclusion in the pot does not automatically mean the other party is entitled to share in the value of these 'assets'.

The factors taken into account to determine the extent to which the compensation, damages or inheritance will be taken into account vary depending on the circumstances of each case.

Kids mean more assets

"Whoever gets the kids after separation gets at least 60 per cent of the assets."

Family law is discretionary, meaning that the courts have wide powers to make orders. Many factors are taken into account to determine how assets will be distributed. Parties' needs will be assessed. Care arrangements for the children are just one of many matters that will be considered. There are no requirements in family law for fixed percentage distributions in any circumstances.

Rather than rely on popular but wildly inaccurate myths, you should seek legal advice about your rights and responsibilities, your entitlements and your obligations at family law. This is the case whether you are separating after a marriage or you are unmarried but living together, whether you are a parent, a grandparent or, simply, a person interested in a child's welfare and development.

THE DO'S AND DON'TS OF DIVORCE

Relationship breakdowns cause considerable emotional distress and upset. Whether you walking out on a relationship or are the one left with a broken heart, such emotions can affect the way we think and can result in unusual and often irrational behaviour.

This vulnerability can also be abused by a bitter spouse, family member or connected individual and can cause considerable embarrassment.

Here's a guide to the do's and don'ts for divorce that should provide a useful guide to anyone facing this difficult time.

The Do's

Forewarned is forearmed

Take advice from a specialist solicitor.

Whether you have been thrown out of the house with nothing but bin bags or left in the house with the children, obtaining advice very often is on the bottom of the priority list. Make it the top priority so that you know what you can and can't do. Knowing where you stand can relieve stress. It is essential that the solicitor is an expert in family law.

Avoid taking advice from friends and family

Whilst they are trying to help and are great as a shoulder to cry on, family and friends tend not to be objective and will often tell you what you want to hear, not what you need to hear. Furthermore, unless they are legally qualified in family law, they are unlikely to able to give you the advice you need and which will protect your best interests.

Obtain valuations

The first thing that anyone facing divorce, and also has a pension, should do is request the Cash Equivalent Transfer Value of his or her pension. This is the value that the courts take into account when considering pension claims. The pension company can take up to 3 months to produce this figure, which can cause considerable delay in negotiations. Also, it will be very difficult to prove to a court the value of a pension at the date of separation if no valuation was obtained. Values of all assets will need to be agreed if possible, so start getting figures together including the surrender value of policies, valuations of property and figures for stocks and shares.

Separate the finances

Separating the family bank accounts not only enables you and your spouse to be independent from each other but also can help reduce the risk of future conflict. It's a good idea for divorcing spouses to open their own bank accounts, have their wage paid into that account and then have a separate account for the payment of bills. Remember, however, that even though you have opened your own bank account, this does not prevent your spouse's solicitor from asking for copies of your statements (even if the account is opened with a new partner).

Pay rent

If you have moved out of the home consider renting a property rather than staying in your mum's back bedroom. Living with the parents rent-free is in some cases going to provide excess income to which a spouse can make a claim.

Communicate

Whilst relations may be tense always try and communicate with your spouse. This not only helps were there are children involved but legal costs can be kept to a minimum. Obviously, in some cases this is not always possible. Even where communication is difficult there are certain events within the divorce process whereupon a quick telephone call can make a difference. For instance, it is always better for a spouse to be told that divorce papers are en route before the brown envelope appears on the doormat.

Seek counselling

Counselling is not for the weak but the wise.

Make a will

Whilst in your mind the marriage is at an end, in the eyes of the law you are still married. Until a will is made your spouse is still your next of kin and is likely to benefit on death.

The Don'ts

Don't do your own detective work

Let someone else play Sherlock Holmes.

If you suspect an affair, avoid undertaking your own surveillance. Following a suspected third party, taking photographs and taping phone calls can leave you in deep water and can be difficult to explain.

Avoid the perils of self-help disclosure

As a marriage breaks down it can be tempting for one party to examine, copy or even retain the other's private documents to learn more about their financial situation. This is a big "no-no". Your spouse has a right to privacy and you will get into serious trouble if you start copying their private documents, hard drives etc. to try and establish what they have. Both of you have a duty to fully disclose your financial position, so wait for them to disclose it and if you think something is missing you can raise a query.

Beware of social networking sites

Millions of people use such sites every day to pass on harmless snippets of gossip to friends and family. Some people, however, use it to publicise where they were at the weekend and happily exhibit photographs of them flirting with members of the opposite sex. A recent survey confirmed that Facebook is referred to in one in five divorce petitions. Remember that even if you have debarred your spouse as a "friend" there, there may be other connections that can spill the beans on anything you have posted.

Don't leave the house before taking advice

Before you leave the family home, consider the implications of doing so. If your partner is in the family home, but you are living in rented accommodation or staying with a friend, they may have no incentive to conclude the divorce, but you may find yourself desperate to do so. If the family home has to be sold as part of the divorce settlement, you may find you have little or no control over ensuring that the house is sold promptly if you are not physically there.

Don't empty the house

If your initial reaction when your marriage breaks down is to grab and run, for fear that you will not be allowed access to those belongings again, then pause and think. Whilst there is nothing to stop you taking what is legally yours, relations with your spouse are likely to plummet significantly.

Beware of quickie divorce sites

There are many websites that promise to bring a speedy divorce at minimum costs. Whilst this may appear to be a cost-effective solution to ending the marriage there can be hidden charges, delays and long-term penalties.

Don't lie to your lawyer - we are on the same side

The best clients are the ones that are straight, want to work with you and more importantly, tell the truth. If the truth is not told, this can lead to mistakes that again can be costly.

Don't empty the joint bank account

Very often people will empty the savings account for fear that their spouse will get there first. If the money is to be used on genuinely required items such as a rent deposit then you are unlikely to be heavily criticised. If the money is spent on a new Ducati motorcycle or a holiday to the Maldives with your new partner, the Judge will not be impressed and is likely to take this conduct into consideration when deciding how the matrimonial assets are to be divided.

Don't be caught out by technology

Open a secure online account; update passwords and security questions; never write them down. Also delete sensitive browsing history and temporary Internet files and password protect any mobile used to access e-mails. Remember that certain web-based products can store confidential documents off your home's PC.

LIFE AFTER DIVORCE, MOVING ON

So, you've come to the end of your journey, you've got your decree absolute in one hand and your Final Order in the other - what next?

People are all different and everyone deals with the end of a relationship in different ways. Some will feel very emotional at what is the end of an era, and others will hold divorce parties.

Here are some of our clients' responses when asked to comment on their experiences on life after divorce:

> *"Looking back now I realise I had already begun to move on from my marriage mentally before divorce proceedings had even started. I had worked so hard at keeping things together that there comes a point when enough is enough and had to act. While I still had a long way to go in working through my feelings of inadequacy and failure at an unsuccessful marriage, the relief of doing something about my unhappy life was one of the few pleasant emotions I had during the early period. If I can recommend one thing to anyone going through divorce is to talk honestly about how you feel, regularly. It really was the only way I was able to understand myself, my patterns of behaviour, why I was unsuccessful in my part of the marriage and ultimately how I was able to move on into a very healthy, very happy relationship."*
>
> *Anon*

> *"Someone once said that divorce is like a bereavement – this is not true, it is actually worse. With a bereavement you still have your memories and photos to remind you of special times. With a divorce those memories become tarnished and in my case, questioned as to whether or not they were actually true. Photos are destroyed as they hold images of lies and double lives, they make you question what you thought had been happy times. Being on my own has, in time, strengthened me. I have abilities I didn't know I had, as you only have yourself to rely on for the every day running of a house and family. I am certainly more independent."*
>
> *Gillian L*

"Divorce is not something to be taken lightly. The ripples continue long after and have far reaching effects – children realise that they have been brainwashed into opinions over time, that what they thought was the truth was not, that they have been made to take one side during a marriage to the detriment of their relationship with one parent. They then reject the parent who has misled them. In my case divorce was the best and worst thing I have ever done. Mixed emotions. Relief that what you realise was pain and abuse will be no more. Pain that what you thought you had was possibly never there, and is certainly irretrievably gone. All in all my life is now peaceful and fairly tranquil. I am, in the main, a happy man. Work is easy now without pressure at home and I realise that I could have easily accomplished a lot more than I have, had I had real support and encouragement. There is an occasional tinge of sadness that I may live out the end of my life alone, but I believe that everything happens for a purpose, and that if I am supposed to meet someone, I will."

Anon

"Within 10 minutes of receiving my decree absolute it was framed and to this day hangs in my downstairs toilet with the words 'less you forget never again!' In my case, although I still have some feelings for my ex, I moved on very quickly. In fact I loved the space I now have which I felt I never had before. I get so much more done. I actually enjoy my own company. All in all I am very content and happy with my lot and think my ex actually did me a big favour."

Stephen K

Whatever feelings you may have, there are people and organisations out there who can help you face your life after separation, here are just a few examples:

- Counsellors.
- Family therapists.
- Image consultants.
- Dating agencies.

Finally, never underestimate the emotional turmoil that a separation can cause. If you're lucky enough to have a good set of friends and/or family around you, then don't be afraid to lean on them for emotional and practical support. In any event, don't be frightened to ask for help from a professional, be it a counsellor or family therapist.

INDEX